SAUCES

over 175 fabulous recipes and cooking ideas

and salsas

CHRISTINE FRANCE

HERMES
HOUSE

This edition published by Hermes House

© Anness Publishing Limited 2000, 2002, 2003

Produced by Anness Publishing Limited
Hermes House
88–89 Blackfriars Road
London SE1 8HA

A CIP catalogue record for this book is available from the British Library.

Publisher: Joanna Lorenz
Project Editor: Simona Hill
Designer: Simon Wilder
Production Controller: Wendy Lawson

Front cover shows Grilled Halibut with a variation of an oil-based dressing for fish, for recipe see page 43

Previously published as *The Complete Book of Sauces, Salsas, Dips, Relishes, Marinades & Dressings*

10 9 8 7 6 5 4 3 2 1

NOTES

Standard spoon and cup measures are level.

Large eggs are used unless otherwise stated

Contents

Introduction

Sauce-making has a reputation for being a difficult art but, in fact, most sauces are simple and can be made in a matter of minutes. True, there are some classic sauces whose preparation takes a little time and a degree of skill, but the skills are easily learned, and you don't have to be a fully trained chef to achieve success.

Once you've mastered a few basic methods and simple techniques, you'll have a collection of sauce recipes always on hand, ready to add a touch of individuality to your cooking, whether for everyday family meals or the most sophisticated dinner parties. Even if you lack the time or skills to cook elaborate dishes, sauces will add originality to your cooking and transform even the plainest dishes into something special.

Sauces can play many different roles in cooking, covering a variety of dishes and almost every occasion. A sauce may be used to complement a dish, add a touch of piquancy, balance flavors or simply enhance the appearance. Others are used to tenderize or moisten foods before and during cooking or to bind ingredients together. Served in the form of a tasty dip or relish, they can give an added dimension to endless snacks and party dishes.

This book gathers together a comprehensive collection of sauces, salsas, dips, relishes, marinades and dressings, from traditional classics to modern ideas, that makes an invaluable reference guide and source of creative ideas for your kitchen.

General Reference

Whether you are a novice cook who wants to add interest and new flavours to weekday meals, or an expert who would like to broaden your repertoire, understanding the basics of sauce-making will provide a firm foundation for a lifetime of creative cooking. Many sauce-making ingredients such as flour and fat are basics in every kitchen. But adding just a few other well-chosen ingredients will provide you with a store cupboard from which to make a whole range of interesting and flavorful accompaniments to meals.

Sauce-making doesn't require any special equipment, and much of what you already own will be sufficient – a selection of pans, bowls, whisks, ladles, sieves, weighing scales and measuring jugs will ensure the correct equipment is always to hand.

The following pages provide a brief explanation of the science behind a successful sauce – which flours to use for a smooth texture, which fats add the best flavor, how much and what type of liquid to use and how to infuse flavors. All the basic methods of sauce-making are included from a classic white sauce to a rich roux and there are plenty of hints and tips to help you produce the best results.

Flours

There is a wide range of flours and thickening agents on the market. It is important to select the right product, since the choice of flour used for a sauce will determine not only the cooking method used, but the final texture and flavor of the finished sauce. These general guidelines should help remove any mystique involved.

WHITE FLOUR

Also known as all-purpose flour, this is the standard choice for making roux-based sauces and gravies. Its fine, smooth texture combines easily with melted fat for a sauce with a roux base, so that when heated, the starch grains burst and cook, thickening the sauce liquid.

White flour usually contains 70–75 percent of the wheat-grain. Most of the bran and wheatgerm have been removed during milling, leaving it almost white, so it is excellent for thickening white sauces. White flour is chemically bleached, making it pale in color and therefore more suitable for white sauces than unbleached, stone-ground flours.

SELF-RISING FLOURS

These are flours designed for specific baking uses, not for sauces, but could be used in an emergency if you run out of plain flour. Self-rising flour has chemical agents added during milling that react with heat to make cake batters rise during cooking.

Below from left to right: Brown flour, whole-wheat flour

Below: Sauce flour

Below: white flour

WHOLE-WHEAT FLOURS

Whole-wheat flours contain more of the bran and wheatgerm, between 80 and 90 percent of the grain, which gives them a nutty flavor and coarse texture and a darker color than white flour. Because of this, they are not usually chosen for making sauces, but if you don't mind the texture and color, there's no reason why any of these flours should not be used for thickening sauces. The bonus is that they will add a little extra dietary fiber and nutrients to the dish.

Below, clockwise from top left: Cornstarch, custard powder, potato flour, arrowroot

CORNSTARCH

This fine ground corn product is a gluten-free starch. It is light and smooth-textured, producing smooth, velvety-textured, lump-free sauces, usually made by the blending method. When first added to a clear liquid it gives a cloudy appearance, but on heating, the sauce becomes almost clear. Because of this, it is a popular choice for Chinese sauces, and its smooth texture makes it particularly suitable for using in sweet white sauces or those that are to be used for coating foods.

POTATO FLOUR

Also known as farine de fécule, potato flour is made from pure potato starch. It is very fine and smooth and is bright white in color. It makes a light, clear thickener for sauces without affecting the flavor. You will need to use slightly less potato flour than ordinary flour for thickening. It is most suited to the blending method of sauce making, and is often used as a thickener in Asian dishes and stir-fry sauces, so it is available at Asian stores.

ARROWROOT

This is a finely ground powder made from the root of a tropical tree, which is grown in Central America. It is used in the same way as cornstarch, for sauces made by the blending method and gives a very smooth, clear, translucent appearance to sweet or savory sauces without affecting either the color or the flavor.

CUSTARD POWDER

A useful thickener for quick custard sauces, this is simply a colored cornstarch-based powder. For a quick custard, a similar result can be achieved by using a small amount of cornstarch with a few drops of yellow food coloring and vanilla. Make into a sauce with milk by the blending method, and sweeten to taste.

STORING FLOUR

Store flour in a cool, dark, dry, airy place, away from steam or dampness. Place the flour in a clean tin or a storage jar with a close-fitting lid, and always make sure you wash and dry the container thoroughly before refilling it. Check the "use by" dates, and use the flour within the recommended date, or replace it. Don't add new flour to old in a storage jar—it is always best to use up the older flour first.

Once opened, white flour can be stored under the right conditions for up to six months, but whole-wheat flours have a higher fat content, so these are best used within two months. Like all food, flour is

best used while fresh. Make sure it is stored in dark, cool conditions; buy it in small amounts and plan to use it quickly rather than storing it indefinitely.

Fats

Fats make sauces palatable and improve the flavor and texture. The ones usually used in sauces are "yellow" fats such as butter margarine and oils. Many are added to cooked sauces as a base with flour, as in a roux, or in beurre manié, where the fat and flour are heated together to cook the starch grains for thickening. The classic emulsified sauces, such as hollandaise or mayonnaise, use either melted butter or liquid oils, beaten with eggs to enrich and thicken to a thick emulsion. The same principle is used in reduced sauces such as beurre blanc, or in oil-based salad dressings such as vinaigrette, where the fat is whisked into a reduced or well-flavored liquid base to make a smooth emulsion. In salsas and purées, oil is added for flavor, being stirred or drizzled onto the ingredients.

TYPES OF FAT

Saturated fats are solid at room temperature, and are the ones that can raise cholesterol levels in the blood. Polyunsaturated fats can help lower cholesterol levels; mono-unsaturated fats, which are beneficial in regulating cholesterol levels, are liquid but can be made solid by a process known as hydrogenation. This is the process used to make margarines and spreads.

BUTTER

A natural product made by churning cream, butter has an 80 percent fat content, which is saturated fat. Butter is made in two basic types, sweet cream and salted. The choice will depend largely on flavor, according to whether you are making a sweet or savory sauce.

Clarified butter, ghee or concentrated butters will with-stand higher temperatures than untreated butter, and will not burn as easily.

Clockwise from top left: Ghee, clarified butter, concentrated butter

MARGARINE

Soft margarines, made from a blend of vegetable oils and/or animal oils, have a soft, spreadable texture. Hard margarines have a firmer texture and are made from animal and vegetable fats. Both types have the same fat content as butter, and can be used as a direct substitute for butter in making sweet and savory sauces. As the flavor is inferior to butter, margarines are best chosen for more robustly flavored sauces where their own flavor will not be as noticeable.

Left: Unsalted butter (left), sweet cream butter

SPREADS

The wide choice of different spreads on the market is confusing to say the least, but as a rough guide, unless they are labeled "low-fat," or "very low-fat," they are generally suitable for sauce-making. After that, choice is very much a matter of personal preference.

Polyunsaturated vegetable oil spreads: Products described in this way are made either from a single vegetable oil or sunflower oil alone, or from a blend of different vegetable oils. They vary in fat content from 61 to 79 percent.

Monounsaturated vegetable oil spreads: Made from olive oil or rapeseed oil, these vary in fat content from 60 to 75 percent.

Dairy spreads: These contain cream or buttermilk to retain a buttery flavor and smooth texture, while providing a lower-fat alternative to butter. The fat content varies between 61 and 75 percent.

Reduced fat spreads: These products are either made from vegetable oils alone or may also contain some dairy or animal fat. Their fat content is between 50 and 60 percent.

Low-fat spreads and very low-fat spreads: These spreads, popular with the weight-conscious, contain less than 40 percent fat and are often as low as 25 percent. They are not recommended for cooking, although they can be added to all-in-one method sauces.

Above, from left: Polyunsaturated, olive, dairy, and reduced-fat spreads

STORING FAT

All solid fats should be stored in the refrigerator, below 39°F. They should be covered or closely wrapped to protect them from light and air. Keep them away from strong-smelling foods, as they can absorb other flavors easily. (The butter storage compartment in most refrigerators is in the door and is not quite so cold as other parts, so the butter should not become too hard.) Oils tend to solidify at low temperatures, so these are best kept in a cool cupboard, but keep them away from light, which will cause them to deteriorate more quickly.

Above: Soft margarine (left) and hard

Right: Very low-fat (left) and low-fat spreads

OILS

These are fats that are liquid at room temperature, and are used in emulsion sauces, such as mayonnaise, or in salad dressings, usually balanced with vinegar or other acids such as citrus juices. However, they can also be used as a direct replacement for butter or hard fats in roux or other flour-thickened sauces, with good results. With the exception of coconut oil and palm oil, they are mostly rich in unsaturated fat, which helps reduce cholesterol levels. The choice of individual oils for a particular sauce depends largely on flavor and personal taste.

Peanut oil: Made from peanuts, this is usually used where a mild flavor is required.

Sesame seed oil: Usually used for flavoring Asian sauces at the end of cooking, as it has an intense, rich flavor and burns easily when heated. However it can be heated with care, or mixed half and half with another oil, such as peanut, if necessary.

Soy oil: A mild flavored oil that will withstand high temperatures, this keeps well and is economical to use.

Sunflower oil: A little more expensive to use than soy oil, this versatile, light-flavored oil is good for sauces or dressings, as it does not mask other flavors.

Nut oils: Walnut and hazelnut oils are the most commonly used nut oils for dressings, lending their rich, distinctive flavors to salads. Use in moderation, perhaps combined with a milder oil, as the flavors can be strong.

OLIVE OILS

The characteristics and quality of olive oils vary and depend on variety, growing region and method of production. Many are blended, but the best quality oils are produced on individual estates. For most sauces, including mayonnaise, it's best to choose virgin or pure olive oil, and keep the more expensive extra virgin ones for salad dressings, or for drizzling directly on foods. It is more economical to buy olive oils in larger amounts.

Extra virgin first pressed or cold pressed olive oils: These oils are made from what is literally the first pressing of the olives, with no additional treatment such as heat or blending. By law, these oils never have more than 1 percent acidity, ensuring a fine flavor. They have a very distinctive flavor, as well as a pungent aroma. They are usually a deep green color and are sometimes cloudy, although both of these factors vary according to the area where the oil has been produced.

Virgin olive oil: This is also cold pressed and unrefined, but has a higher acidity content than extra virgin oil, with a maximum level of 1 to 1.5 percent.

Pure olive oil: This comes from the third or fourth pressing of the olives, and is usually blended. It has a maximum acid content of 2 percent. It is widely used in cooking, since it is not overpowering.

Light olive oil: This is from the last pressing of the fruit and has the lightest flavor of all.

Below, from left: Peanut oil, sunflower oil, soy oil, sesame oil, walnut oil

The Pantry

A well-stocked pantry makes every cook's life a lot easier, and when it comes to sauce making, it really makes sense. Just by keeping a few basic ingredients on hand, you will always be able to whip up an impromptu sauce when the occasion demands, transforming a simple dish into something really special.

BOUILLON CUBES AND POWDERS

There is a wide range of commercial bouillon cubes and powders on the market, and these vary in flavor and quality. Good-quality products make adequate substitutes for fresh stock, and certainly they are very convenient to use. However, some tend to be quite salty, so allow for this when adding other seasonings. Follow the package directions. Generally speaking, it is worth paying a little more for good-quality bouillon cubes or powder, and it is worth choosing one that is made with natural ingredients, which should impart a more natural flavor.

Many supermarkets also now sell ready-made cartons of basic fresh stocks in the refrigerated food section, such as

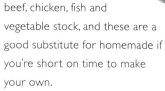

beef, chicken, fish and vegetable stock, and these are a good substitute for homemade if you're short on time to make your own.

Canned consommé makes an excellent substitute for a good brown stock in rich savory sauces, so is well worth keeping on hand. If you need a light stock, the color of consommé may be too dark, but brands vary.

CANNED TOMATOES AND SAUCES

Since many of the plum tomatoes we buy out of season in this country are lacking in flavor, it's a safer bet to go for good-quality canned tomatoes in recipes, either whole or chopped. The best are from Italy, so check the label carefully. *Polpa di pomodoro* are finely chopped or crushed. Avoid those

with added herbs or spices, which are best added fresh.

Above: Consommé
Left: Bouillon cubes and powder
Below, clockwise from left: Passata, sugocasa, whole plum tomatoes, tomato paste, chopped tomatoes

Crushed or puréed tomatoes: Sold as sugocasa, polpa and passata, and usually packed in convenient jars or bottles, these are invaluable for sauces. Sugocasa and polpa have a chunky texture, and passata is sieved to a smooth purée.

Tomato paste: This is concentrated, cooked tomato pulp in a strong, thick paste, and is sold in tubes or cans. The strength of different brands varies, so use with care or the flavor can overpower a sauce. Sun-dried tomato paste is a purée of sun-dried tomatoes with olive oil. It has a sweet, rich flavor, and is milder than ordinary tomato paste.

Below, top row from left: Oyster sauce, soy sauce, Worcestershire sauce, fish sauce, hot pepper sauce. Bottom row: Red pesto, green pesto, English mustard

COOK'S TIP

Chopped canned tomatoes are usually more expensive than whole ones, so you can save valuable pennies by simply chopping them yourself.

COMMERCIAL SAUCES

The huge range of commercially-made flavoring sauces now available is a boon to the creative cook. Some of the most useful ones to keep in your pantry are:

Hot pepper sauces: Widely used in West Indian and South American cooking, there are many versions of pepper sauce, the most famous being Tabasco. Use with caution, as they can be fiery hot. These sauces will pep up the flavor of almost any savory sauce, marinade or dressing.

Mustards: Ready-made mustards are a blend of ground mustard seeds with flour and salt, often with wine, herbs and other spices. Dijon is often used for classic French sauces and for dressings such as vinaigrette and mayonnaise—it also helps to stabilize the emulsion. Yellow English mustard is a good choice to give color and bite to cheese sauce or to flavor rich gravies for meat. Milder German mustard is good for a barbecue sauce to serve with chops or sausages. Mild, creamy yellow mustard is squeezed on hotdogs or burgers. Whole-grain mustard gives a pleasant texture, particularly to creamy savory sauces and dressings.

Oyster sauce: A thicker-textured sauce made with the extract of real oysters, this adds a delicious sweet-savory flavor to sauces for accompanying meat, fish or vegetables.

Pesto: Commercially made pesto is sold as either the traditional green basil pesto or a red pesto made from sun-dried tomatoes. Use it just as it is as a replacement for fresh pesto to stir into pasta, pepped up with a little freshly grated Parmesan cheese or an extra drizzle of olive oil. You can also add it by the spoonful to enrich and enhance the flavor of tomato sauces, salsas and

Coconut Milk and Cream

Coconut milk and cream are used widely in Asian dishes, particularly those based on spicy and curried sauces. They can be used much like dairy products, for thickening, enriching and flavoring.

Coconut milk: This is available in cans and packages. It is similar in thickness to light cream.

Coconut cream: This has the thickness of heavy cream. Creamed coconut is solid and white; it is sold in solid blocks, so you can cut off just the amount you need and melt it into sauces. Creamed coconut can be found in some gourmet markets.

Right, clockwise from left: Coconut cream, coconut milk, creamed coconut

dressings. Once the jar is opened, it should be treated as fresh and stored in the refrigerator.

Soy sauce: Although this is traditionally used with Chinese and Japanese foods, there is no need to limit its use to Asian dishes. Use it to flavor and color all kinds of savory sauces, marinades and dressings. Light soy sauce is good in light, sweet-and-sour or stir-fry sauces for fish or vegetables, and the richer, sweeter dark soy sauce is best with rich meat sauces such as satés, or for barbecue sauces.

Thai fish sauce or *nam pla*: This is a classic Thai sauce made from fermented fish. It has a pungent flavor and is best in cooked sauces. It adds richness to sauces for both meat and fish.

Worcestershire sauce: This classic English sauce has its origins in India. Its spicy, mellowed flavor enhances savory sauces, marinades and dressings of any type.

VINEGARS

These are made from alcoholic bases of malt, wine, beer, cider, rice wine and sugar, and most of these can be used to enhance flavor in sauces or as emulsifiers. Red and white wine vinegars and fruit vinegars are particularly useful

for salad dressings, and rice vinegars add authentic flavors to Asian sauces. When using some of the dark, long-aged sherry or balsamic vinegars, bear in mind that they often have intense, powerful flavors and you may only need a few drops.

Below, from left: Balsamic vinegar, white wine vinegar, red wine vinegar, raspberry vinegar

Herbs and Spices

Many sauce recipes call for herbs and spices to add flavor and color, and there's no end to the variety you can buy nowadays, especially at the larger supermarkets and good Asian grocers. Generally speaking, herbs are the leafy tops and stems of an edible plant, and spices are from the berries, seeds, bark, and roots.

CULINARY HERBS

It's worth growing a few of the more useful common herbs yourself. Some herbs grown in pots on the kitchen windowsill, will always be handy when you need to snip off a few sprigs. It is considerably cheaper, too, as packaged fresh herbs have a limited life and can be quite costly. A useful basic selection to grow at home would include parsley, chives, thyme, mint, oregano, sage, bay and dill.

When cooking with herbs, you don't need to be too precise. Treat the measurements quoted in recipes as a general guide, and add the herbs according to your personal preference.

DRIED AND FROZEN HERBS

Dried herbs are useful to keep on hand for emergencies, but always choose fresh if you can get them. Many of the delicate-leaved herbs, such as basil, cilantro or chervil, do not dry successfully, but the ones that are worth buying dried are

Above, clockwise from top left: Chopped and frozen herbs – coriander, parsley, chives

thyme, rosemary, parsley, mint, oregano, tarragon and dill. Store dried herbs in airtight containers in a cool place away from light, and use them quickly, as their flavor is soon lost.

Frozen herbs, such as parsley, chives and cilantro, retain more of the flavor of fresh herbs and can be very useful and convenient—they can be added to a sauce or dressing right from the freezer.

SALT AND PEPPER

Good-quality sea salt has a more intense flavor than "table" or "cooking" salt. Strong black peppercorns, mild white and very mild green are all worth storing.

Below, clockwise from bowl: Tandoori curry paste, nutmeg, cinnamon sticks, vanilla beans, salt, whole coriander, cumin seeds, black, green, white peppercorns

Above, clockwise from left: Mint, bay, thyme

Above, clockwise from top: Freeze-dried mint, freeze-dried parsley, freeze-dried dill, freeze-dried tarragon, dried thyme, dried rosemary. Center: Freeze-dried oregano

SPICES

Keep a good store of spices in the kitchen. A useful selection includes whole nutmeg, cinnamon sticks, vanilla beans, coriander seeds, cumin seeds and curry paste (curry pastes keep for much longer than powders).

Cinnamon sticks: These have a sweet, spicy flavor and are widely used in sweet sauces and chutneys. They can either be crushed or used whole and removed at the end of cooking.

Coriander: These seeds are used in chutneys and have a mild sweet flavor.

Cumin: A key ingredient in chutneys and curries, these seeds have a strong and slightly bitter taste.

Curry paste: This is sold in a range of strengths and flavors. It keeps for much longer than curry powder.

Vanilla beans: Infuse these dried beans in milk or cream for sweet sauces and custards. Store in a jar of sugar to make vanilla sugar.

Whole nutmeg: Freshly grated whole nutmeg is much better than the powdered variety, which quickly loses its flavor.

STORING SPICES

Whole spices will store for much longer than ready-ground ones and have a stronger, more intense flavor. Once ground, they begin to lose the volatile oils that give them flavor, so it is best to grind whole spices yourself, either in a mortar and pestle or with a spice mill or using an electric coffee grinder. Buy them often and store in airtight containers in a cool, dark, dry cupboard. Discard any that have not been used after a year.

Extracts and Flower Waters

Vanilla or other flavoring extracts can be very convenient, but choose carefully, as some are inferior artificial flavorings. Check the label—it should describe the contents as pure vanilla extract, not vanilla flavoring.

Flower waters are a delightful way to flavor cold sweet sauces, syrups and creams in particular, but occasionally they are used in Middle Eastern savory sauces. The best known are rose and orange flower water, and should be used in small amounts—the best quality flower waters are triple-distilled, so just a few drops will add a delicately exotic scent to a creamy sauce.

Right, from left: Flower essences, vanilla extract, almond extract

Dairy Products

The number of sauces based on dairy products is vast, so it is worth taking the time to understand the different products available. You may be aiming for a rich and creamy sauce, or perhaps you would prefer a lighter, healthier alternative. The following descriptions should help.

MILK

The choice of milk for sauces depends on the richness desired—for a rich flavor and creamy texture, choose whole milk, but if you're watching fat levels and looking for a lighter sauce, it is best to go for low-fat or skim.

Pasteurized: Most milk sold these days has been pasteurized, i.e. heat-treated, to destroy harmful bacteria. This should keep for up to 5 days under refrigeration.

Homogenized: This has been processed to distribute the fat globules evenly throughout the milk, instead of rising to the surface as cream. It has the same keeping quality as ordinary milk.

Sterilized: This is homogenized, bottled and then heat-treated for 20 minutes, so that it keeps without refrigeration until it is opened.

UHT: This is homogenized then heat-treated to high temperatures for just 1–2 seconds. It has a slightly caramelized flavor, but is useful as a staple, as it keeps unopened for about a year without refrigeration.

Condensed: This sweetened milk is available in cans, and has been boiled to reduce and concentrate it. It is very rich and sweet but useful for rich dessert sauces. Lower-fat versions are available.

Evaporated: Unsweetened milk that has had some of the water removed by evaporation, this milk has a concentrated flavor and is slightly caramelized. There are also lighter-fat versions available. It is available either in cans or longlife packages.

Goat's milk: Many people who are allergic to cow's milk can tolerate goat's milk, which is now widely available and can be used as a direct substitute for ordinary milk in cooking. It has a similar flavor, although it is slightly sharper and is more digestible.

CREAM

All kinds of creams can be used to enrich and thicken both sweet and savory sauces, both hot and cold. The main ones are as follows:

Light cream: This cream has a fat content of just 18 percent, which is too low for whipping. It will not withstand boiling without separating, but can be stirred into sauces at the end of cooking to enrich the flavor.

Sour cream: This is really light cream with an added souring culture, which sharpens the flavor and thickens the texture.

Heavy cream: The fat content of heavy cream is 48 percent. The cream almost doubles in bulk when whipped. It is espe-

cially good in hot sauces, because it can withstand boiling without separating.

Whipping cream: This has 35 percent fat, and whips up to a light texture or can be stirred into sauces after cooking.

Fat Levels in Milk

- Whole milk: 4 percent fat
- Low-fat: 1.7 percent fat
- Skim: 0.1 percent fat

COOK'S TIP

When whipping heavy cream, you can reduce the risk of overbeating and extend the volume by adding 1 tablespoon milk to each ⅔ cup cream. Use a hand whisk instead of an electric one, so you have more control over the speed.

CRÈME FRAÎCHE

This has a mild, tangy flavor similar to that of sour cream, which makes it great for using in both sweet and savory sauces and dressings. With a fat content of around

Below, from left: Skim milk, low-fat milk, whole milk, whole enriched milk, evaporated milk, condensed milk

40 percent, it is more stable than sour cream when heated. You can also buy a low-fat version, which can be successfully added to hot sauces without curdling.

Above, clockwise from left: Light cream, heavy cream, crème fraîche, sour cream, whipping cream

YOGURT

Yogurt and other lower-fat dairy products such as fromage frais, make excellent lighter replacements for cream in many sweet and savory sauces, and can be used as a direct substitute to add a lighter tang to all kinds of uncooked sauces. For cooked sauces, yogurt should be stabilized first with cornstarch.

Plain yogurt: This may be made from either cow's or sheep's milk. It is richer in flavor and texture than low-fat yogurts, but still only has a fat content of around 8–10 percent, so it makes a light substitute for cream in sauces.

Low-fat yogurt: It is the use of low-fat milk that makes this yogurt low-fat. Very low-fat yogurt is made with skim milk. Both types have quite a sharp, tangy flavor that can be refreshing when used in light sauces, dips and dressings.

Above: Plain yogurt (left), low-fat yogurt

STABILIZING YOGURT FOR SAUCES

To prevent yogurt from separating in cooked sauces, allow 1 teaspoon cornstarch to each ⅔ cup yogurt. Blend the cornstarch and a little yogurt into a smooth paste before adding the rest. Add to the sauce and cook as instructed in the recipe.

Above: Eggs

CHEESE

Many hard cheeses can be grated and melted into sauces. Strong, hard cheeses such as aged Cheddar, Gruyère and Parmesan will grate easily and melt into hot sauces. Their fine flavor complements pasta sauces or a creamy white sauce to pour over vegetables. Always grate these cheeses freshly as you need them, and never use ready-grated Parmesan, as the flavor is soon lost after grating. Once you've added cheese to a sauce, heat it gently without boiling, or the cheese will overcook and become stringy.

Soft, fresh cheeses such as ricotta or mascarpone are also used to enrich a wide range of sauces and dips, from tomato sauces to fruit purées or custards. Ricotta is light in texture and mild in flavor, and makes a good base for dips instead of yogurt, or can be melted into hot sauces. Mascarpone has a luxuriously rich texture, creamy and high in fat, and can be used in the same way as thick cream.

Below, clockwise from top: Parmesan, mascarpone, ricotta, Cheddar, Gruyère

EGGS

As a general rule, medium eggs are the size to use for recipes, unless the recipe states otherwise, but you may find it useful to have small eggs for using to enrich or thicken sauces.

The freshness of eggs is easier to ensure nowadays, as most are now individually marked with a date stamp on their shells. Fresh eggs should keep well for 2 weeks, providing the shell is not damaged or dirty. Egg shells are porous, so they are best stored at the bottom of the refrigerator away from strong smelling foods. Before use, eggs should be left at room temperature for about 30 minutes.

SAFETY TIP

Because of the slight risk of contamination in raw eggs, it is recommended that pregnant women, young children, elderly people or anyone weakened by chronic illness should avoid eating raw or lightly cooked eggs.

Sauce-making Equipment

Making sauces requires very little in the way of specialty equipment, but a carefully selected set of basic equipment will help make tasks such as boiling, whisking and straining much easier. You may even find that most of these items are already in your kitchen. Shop around for those you still need, as quality varies enormously.

SAUCEPANS

The rule here is to choose the right pan for the job, which means that your saucepans do not necessarily have to be a matching set. Some pans may be suitable for more than one task, but you will need a variety of sizes and types. Look for solid, heavy pans that are stable when empty, and have tight-fitting lids and firmly riveted handles. Buying good-quality pans is an investment, as they will last for years, but cheap, thin pans will not only wear out quickly, but will conduct heat unevenly and cause burned spots. A good selection would be:

• Pan with high sides and a lip. This may be nonstick, but that is not essential.

• 3 saucepans with lids, ranging in size from about 4 cups to 30 cups. They should be deep and straight-sided to minimize evaporation.

• Sauté pan with deep, straight sides.

• Double boiler—a useful pan for making delicate custards and melting ingredients such as chocolate. If you don't have one, improvise with a heatproof bowl placed over a pan of hot water.

MATERIALS FOR SAUCEPANS

Stainless steel: This is attractive and hard-wearing and, providing they have a thick base with aluminum or copper, the pans will conduct heat evenly and efficiently.

Anodized aluminum: Light and easy to clean, this conducts heat well and does not corrode. The metal reacts when in contact with acid and alkaline, so food should not be left to stand for too long in these pans.

Copper: These pans are expensive but conduct heat very efficiently and

Top: Double boiler and heatproof bowl placed over pan
Right, clockwise from left: Enameled, anodized aluminum and copper pans

Above, from left: Spiral sauce whisks, balloon whisk, wooden spoons

are attractive and durable. Choose pans with a stainless steel lining, which is harder-wearing than tin.

Enameled cast iron: This is heavy, but conducts the heat well, evenly and slowly. These pans retain the heat for a long time, and are hard-wearing and durable.

WOODEN SPOONS

A good assortment of wooden spoons is essential, and it is a good idea to keep them for individual uses. For example, you might reserve one for spicy sauces, one for creams and custards, and so on; then there is no risk of flavor transfer. A good selection includes a wooden spoon, a wooden corner spoon with an edge to reach into the corners of saucepans, and a flat-edged wooden spatula, for efficient stirring without scratching.

WHISKS

Balloon whisks and spiral sauce whisks are the most efficient for blending sauce ingredients or whisking dressings, and it is useful to have two different sizes. Choose ones with a comfortable grip.

LADLES

Available in various sizes, ladles are very useful for spooning and pouring sauces over foods. Some smaller ones have a useful lip for more precise pouring. Stainless steel ladles are the best. A slotted stainless steel draining spoon is invaluable for skimming and removing small pieces of ingredients from sauces.

Bottom, from left: Draining spoon, ladles

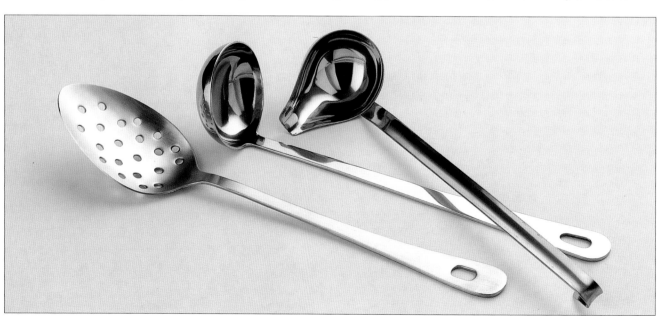

MEASURING CUP

Choose a solid cup marked clearly with standard measurements. Heatproof glass is ideal, as it is easy to see the liquid level and can take boiling liquids, yet the handle remains cool, as it is a poor conductor of heat. Stainless steel cups are attractive and hard-wearing.

MEASURING SPOONS

A set of measuring spoons is essential for accurate measuring of small amounts of sauce ingredients, as ordinary kitchen

Below, from top: Hand-held electric beater, hand blender
Right, from top: Sieve and chinois, measuring cup and spoons

spoons vary in capacity. Spoon measurements given in recipes are always level.

SIEVE AND CHINOIS

A fine-meshed stainless steel sieve is essential for sauce making, and it can also be very useful to have a chinois, a cone-shaped sieve that is used for straining and puréeing a range of ingredients.

ELECTRICAL EQUIPMENT

Although not essential for making sauces, a blender, food processor, hand blender or whisk can take much of the hard work out of many sauces and dressings. Hand-held electric blenders are perhaps more versatile and convenient than

larger machines for sauces, as they can be used to blend or purée ingredients directly in a saucepan or jug, and are easy to clean by simply swishing in hot soapy water after use. A hand-held electric beater is also invaluable for quick and easy beating and whisking.

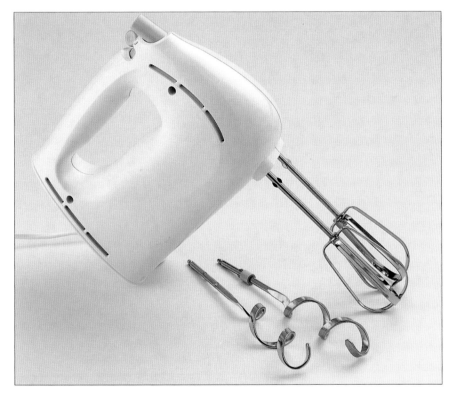

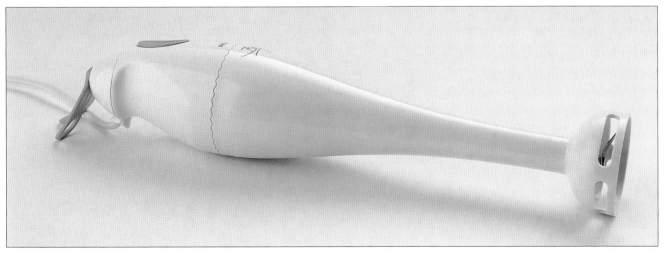

Making Basic Stocks

A good homemade stock is simple to make and adds a rich flavor to all kinds of savory sauces. Commercial bouillon cubes won't match the flavor of homemade stock. However, they can be very useful for enriching a stock that lacks flavor: heat it until boiling, then stir in a bouillon cube until dissolved. Each recipe below makes approximately 4 cups.

Beef Stock

INGREDIENTS

1½ pounds shin of beef, diced
1 large onion, chopped
1 large carrot, chopped
1 celery stalk, chopped
bouquet garni
6 black peppercorns
½ teaspoon sea salt
7½ cups water

1 | Place all the ingredients in a large pan and slowly bring to a boil.

2 | Cover the pan and simmer very gently for 4 hours, skimming occasionally to remove scum. Strain the stock and cool.

Fish Stock

INGREDIENTS

2¼ pounds white fish bones and trimmings
1 large onion, sliced
1 large carrot, sliced
1 celery stalk, sliced
bouquet garni
6 white peppercorns
½ teaspoon sea salt
⅔ cup dry white wine
4 cups water

1 | Place the ingredients in a pan and bring to a boil.

2 | Skim any scum from the surface, cover the pan and simmer for 20 minutes. Strain and let cool.

Chicken Stock

INGREDIENTS

1 chicken carcass
chicken giblets
1 leek, chopped
1 celery stalk, chopped
bouquet garni
1 teaspoon white peppercorns
½ teaspoon sea salt
7½ cups water

1 | Break up the carcass, place in a pan with the remaining ingredients. Bring to a boil.

2 | Reduce the heat, cover and simmer gently for about 2½ hours, skimming occasionally to remove scum. Strain the stock and cool.

Vegetable Stock

INGREDIENTS

1¼ pounds chopped mixed vegetables, e.g. onions, carrots, celery, leeks
bouquet garni
6 black peppercorns
½ teaspoon sea salt
4 cups water

1 | Place all the ingredients in a large pan and slowly bring to a boil.

2 | Skim any scum from the surface, then cover the pan and simmer gently for 30 minutes. Strain the stock and let cool.

Making a Bouquet Garni

A traditional bouquet garni usually contains a bay leaf, a sprig of thyme and a few sprigs of parsley, but this can be varied according to taste, and to suit the dish you are making. Other vegetables or herbs you may like to include are a piece of celery for poultry dishes; a rosemary sprig for beef or lamb; or a piece of fennel or leek, or a strip of lemon zest, to flavor fish dishes.

Tie the herbs together firmly with fine cotton string, so the bundle is easy to remove from the stock after cooking.

Alternatively, tie the herbs in a square of clean muslin. Leave a long length of the string to tie to the pan handle.

Keeping Stock Clear

For a clear soup it is important to keep the stock clear; avoid boiling the soup, and skim the top from time to time.

1 Trim any fat from the meat or bones before adding to the stock pan, as this can create a cloudy stock.

2 Keep the heat at a low simmer, and skim off any scum as it gathers on the surface during cooking. Most vegetables can be added to stock for flavor, but potatoes tend to break down and make the stock cloudy, so it's best to avoid these.

3 Strain the cooked stock through a sieve lined with muslin, and avoid pressing the solids, as this may spoil the stock's clarity.

Removing Fat from Stock

Excess fat should always be removed from the liquid to improve the look and taste of the stock; it also helps keep the stock clear.

1 Let the stock stand until the fat settles on the surface, then skim off as much fat as possible with a large, shallow spoon. To absorb even more grease, blot the surface of the soup with several layers of paper towels.

2 Then, drop in a few ice cubes. The fat will set around the ice so it can be simply spooned off.

3 Alternatively, let the stock cool on a work surface, then chill in the refrigerator until the fat layer rises to the surface and sets. Then the fat can simply be lifted off. Use a large spoon to remove the solidified fat and discard it.

How to Store Stock

Stock will keep for up to a week in the refrigerator, and freezes well. Reduce it first so that it takes up less room in the freezer.

1 To freeze, pour into airtight containers, allowing 1-inch headspace for expansion, then seal and freeze for up to 3 months.

2 To freeze stock in convenient portions to add to sauces, pour into ice cube trays for freezing.

COOK'S TIP

• *Use salt sparingly at the beginning of cooking—if you are going to reduce the stock it will become much more salty.*

• *To make a brown stock from beef or veal bones, roast the bones in a hot oven for 40 minutes. Add the vegetables halfway through the roasting time. Deglaze the pan with a little water and simmer the bones and vegetables as usual.*

• *To make a stock with a concentrated flavor, simmer the stock until reduced by half. Continue to reduce the stock until it will coat the back of a spoon. At its most concentrated it will set as a solid jelly and give you a quick and easy way to add rich flavor to sauces and soups.*

Flour-based Sauces

The standard way to adjust the consistency of a sauce is to thicken it with one of the different available types of flour. There are three basic methods for this—roux, blending or all-in-one. Once you've learned the basic skills of these methods, you'll be able to tackle any flour-thickened sauce without problems.

Many of the classic white sauces are based on a "roux," which is simply a cooked mixture of flour and fat. The most basic white sauce uses milk, but by varying the liquid used other well-known white sauces can be made. For a classic béchamel sauce, the milk is flavored first by infusing with pieces of vegetables and herbs. For velouté sauce, the milk is replaced with stock, giving the sauce a more opaque appearance, and the thickened sauce may be enriched with cream after cooking. Brown sauces or gravy are made by browning the roux, usually with onions, before adding stock or other liquid such as wine.

Basic Recipe for White Roux Sauces

Using the classic roux method, you can adjust the amount of thickening to create varying consistencies of sauces. A pouring sauce is used, as it suggests, to be poured directly onto foods when serving. The slightly thicker coating sauce is used to make a smooth covering for fish or vegetables.

For a pouring consistency:
1 tablespoon butter
2 tablespoons all-purpose flour
1¼ cups liquid

For a coating consistency:
2 tablespoons butter
¼ cup all-purpose flour
1¼ cups liquid

Making a Roux-based White Sauce

The trick to making a roux is to stir constantly, and add the liquid gradually; it is a good idea to heat the milk or stock before adding to the roux, as this helps avoid lumps.

Melt the butter in a saucepan, then add the flour. To prevent browning, cook over low heat and stir with a wooden spoon, for 1–2 minutes. Let the mixture bubble until it resembles a honeycomb in texture. It is important to cook well at this point, to let the starch grains in the flour swell and burst, and avoid having lumps form later.

2 Remove the pan from heat and gradually stir in the liquid, which may be either hot or cold. Return to the heat and stir until boiling and thickened. Reduce the heat and simmer, stirring constantly, for 2 minutes, until the sauce is thickened and smooth.

Blending Method

Sauces that are thickened by the blending method are usually made with cornstarch, arrowroot, or potato starch or flour. Cornstarch and flour make light, glossy, lump-free sauces, which are good for freezing, as the starch does not break down. If you need a crystal-clear result for glazing, use arrowroot or potato starch. The liquid may be milk, stock, fruit juice or syrup from canned or poached fruit. As an approximate guide, you will need 3 tablespoons cornstarch or flour to thicken 1¼ cups liquid to a pouring consistency. Arrowroot or potato starch are slightly stronger, so use approximately ½ ounce to 1¼ cups liquid to obtain the same consistency.

Place the flour in a bowl and add just enough liquid to make a smooth, thin paste. Heat the remaining liquid in a saucepan until almost boiling.

2 Pour a little of the liquid onto the blended mixture, stirring. Pour the blended mixture back into the pan, whisking constantly to avoid lumps. Return to the heat and stir until boiling, then simmer gently for 2 minutes, stirring until thickened and smooth.

All-in-one Method

This method uses the same ingredients and proportions as the roux method, but the liquid added must be cold.

Place the flour, butter and cold liquid in the saucepan and whisk with a sauce whisk or balloon whisk over medium heat until boiling. Stir over the heat for 2 minutes, until thickened and smooth.

Using an Egg Yolk Liaison

This is a simple way to lightly thicken hot milk or stock, cream or reduced poaching liquids, and is good for enriching savory white or velouté sauces. Two egg yolks should be enough to enrich and thicken about 1¼ cups liquid, depending on the recipe. A mixture of egg yolk and cream has the same effect, but add it when the pan is off the heat to avoid curdling.

Place two egg yolks in a small bowl and stir in 2 tablespoons of the hot liquid or sauce. Stir the egg mixture into the remaining liquid or sauce and heat gently, stirring, without boiling.

Making Beurre Manié

Literally translated as "kneaded butter," this is a mixture of flour and butter, which can be stirred into a hot sauce, poaching liquid or cooked dish such as a casserole or ragout to thicken the juices. It's a convenient way to adjust the consistency of a sauce or dish at the end of cooking and is easy to control, as you can add the exact amount required, adjusting as it thickens. The butter adds flavor and a glossy sheen to the finished sauce. Any leftover beurre manié can be stored in a covered jar in the refrigerator for about two weeks, ready to use in sauces, soups, stews or casseroles.

1 Place equal amounts of butter and flour in a bowl and knead together with your fingers or a wooden spoon to make a smooth paste.

2 Drop teaspoonfuls of the beurre manié paste into the simmering sauce, whisking thoroughly to incorporate each spoonful before adding the next, until the sauce is thickened and smooth and the desired consistency is achieved.

Infusing Flavors

To infuse flavors into milk, stock or other liquids before using in sauces such as béchamel, pour the liquid into a saucepan and add thin slices or dice of onion, carrot and celery, a bouquet garni, peppercorns or a mace blade. Bring the liquid slowly to a boil, then remove the pan from heat. Cover and let stand for about 10 minutes. Strain the milk to remove the flavorings before use.

Adding Flavorings to Flour-based Sauces

Once you've made your basic sauce, try some of these quick flavor additions to pep up the flavor and add variety:
• Stir ½ cup grated Cheddar or other strong cheese into a basic white sauce with 1 teaspoon whole-grain mustard and a generous dash of Worcestershire sauce.
• Wine enlivens the flavor of most stock-based sauces—boil 4 tablespoons red or white wine in a saucepan until well-reduced, then stir into the finished sauce with a grating of nutmeg or black pepper.
• Parsley, or any fresh herbs will infuse and change the flavor of a white sauce. Add chopped herbs a few minutes before the end of the cooking time.

Correcting a Lumpy Sauce

If your flour-thickened sauce is lumpy, don't despair—it can be corrected.

| First, try whisking the sauce hard with a light wire whisk in the saucepan to smooth out the lumps, then reheat gently, stirring.

2 If the sauce is still not smooth, rub it through a fine sieve, pressing firmly with a wooden spoon. Return to the pan and reheat gently, stirring.

3 Alternatively, pour the sauce into a food processor and process until smooth. Return to the pan and reheat gently, stirring.

Keeping Sauces Hot

| To keep sauces hot, pour into a heatproof bowl and place over a pan of very gently simmering water.

2 To prevent a skin from forming over the surface, place a sheet of lightly oiled or wetted waxed or nonstick baking parchment directly onto the surface of the sauce. Stir before serving.

Degreasing Sauces

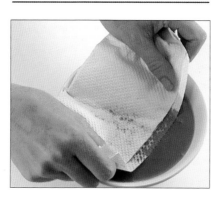

Even after skimming any surplus fat from a finished hot sauce or gravy with a flat metal spoon, final traces of fat may still remain. These can be removed by dragging the flat surface of a piece of paper towel over the surface to absorb traces of grease.

Making a Roux-based Brown Sauce

A brown roux is the basis of many meat dish sauces. Onions or other vegetables are usually browned in fat before flour is added. The fat can be a mixture of butter and oil, or dripping. Butter alone is unsuitable as it burns easily at high temperatures. Use about 2 tablespoons oil and about ¼ cup flour for the roux to about 2½ cups reduced brown stock. At the last moment, stir in 1 tablespoon chilled butter to give a glossy finish.

| Melt the fat and fry one small, finely chopped onion until softened and golden brown. Sprinkle on the flour and stir in with a wooden spoon. Stir over low heat for 4–5 minutes, until the mixture colors to a rich brown.

2 Remove the pan from heat and gradually stir in the liquid, which may be either hot or cold. Return to the heat and stir until boiling. Simmer gently, stirring, for another 2 minutes, until the sauce is thick and smooth. The sauce may be strained to remove the onions at this stage if preferred.

Using a Deglazed Sauce

Deglazing means adding a small amount of liquid to the pan after roasting or pan-frying to dilute the rich concentrated juices into a simple sauce. Spoon off the excess fat, and then scrape up the sediment from the bottom of the pan with a spoon as you stir in the liquid.

Tilt the pan and spoon off excess fat from the surface of the juices.

2 Stir in a few tablespoons of wine, stock or cream.

3 Simmer over medium heat, stirring and scraping up the sediment as the sauce boils. Boil rapidly to reduce the juices until syrupy, then pour onto the food.

Making Traditional Gravy

Good gravy should be smooth and glossy, never heavy and floury. Generally speaking, it's best to use the minimum of thickening, but this can be adjusted to your own taste. Providing the meat has been roasted to a rich brown, the meat juices will have enough color to color the gravy. If it is too pale, a few drops of gravy browning can be stirred in to darken it slightly.

To make a thickened gravy, skim of all except about 1 tablespoon of the fat from the juices in the pan after roasting meat. Gradually stir in about 1 tablespoon flour, scraping up the sediment and meat juices.

2 Place the pan directly over the heat and stir until bubbling. Cook, stirring constantly, for 1–2 minutes, until the roux is brown and the flour cooked.

3 Gradually stir in the liquid, which may be either stock or vegetable water, until the gravy is of the thickness desired. Simmer for 2–3 minutes, stirring constantly, and adjust the seasoning to taste.

Ideas for Deglazed Sauces

Brandy and Peppercorn—deglaze the pan with brandy or sherry, stir in cream and coarsely ground black pepper. Serve with steak.

Red Wine and Cranberry—deglaze the pan with red wine and stir in cranberry sauce or jelly. This recipe is good with roast game or turkey.

Sauce Bercy—deglaze with dry white wine or vermouth, stir in a finely chopped shallot and sauté gently until soft. Add cream, lemon juice and chopped parsley. Excellent with fried or poached fish.

Adding Flavorings to a Brown Sauce

A well-flavored brown stock, which has been reduced by between one-third to a half, is the basis of a good brown sauce but it can also be enhanced by the addition of a variety of flavorings.

• A handful of chopped fresh basil, chives or flat-leaf parsley, stirred into the sauce just before serving, will improve the flavor and look of a basic brown sauce.

• For game or poultry, stir a little curry paste, 2 crushed cloves of garlic and 1 finely chopped onion into the roux and cook for about 5 minutes before adding the stock. Stir in a handful of chopped cilantro just before serving.

• Add coarsely grated orange zest to a basic brown sauce and serve it with duck or game.

Vegetable Sauces and Salsas

Many sauces use vegetables for flavor, color and texture, and there's no end to the healthy variations you can make with a few very simple techniques. Puréed or chopped vegetables can be used to make both cooked sauces and fresh salsas. Vegetable sauces and salsas make fresh, colorful, low-fat alternatives to more conventional sauces, and they are invariably very easy and quick to make.

Basic Tomato Sauce

For the best flavor, use plum tomatoes. If using canned, make sure they are not already flavored with herbs. Peel fresh tomatoes before using. Fresh tomatoes rather than canned tomatoes can be used. Substitute about 1¼ pounds of tomatoes for each 14-ounce can.

Makes a scant 2 cups

INGREDIENTS

1 tablespoon olive oil
1 tablespoon butter
1 clove garlic, finely chopped
1 small onion, finely chopped
1 celery stalk, finely chopped
14-ounce can chopped tomatoes
handful of basil leaves
salt and ground black pepper

1 Heat the oil and butter in a heavy saucepan.

2 When the oil starts to bubble, add the garlic, onion and celery. Sauté the ingredients gently over low heat, stirring occasionally, for 15–20 minutes or until the onions soften and are just beginning to color.

3 Stir the chopped tomatoes into the sauce and bring to a boil. Cover and simmer gently for 10–15 minutes, stirring occasionally, until thick.

4 Tear or roughly chop the basil leaves and stir into the sauce. Adjust the seasoning with salt and pepper and serve hot.

COOK'S TIP

A soffritto (Italian), or sofrito (Spanish), is the basis of many Mediterranean meat or tomato sauces. It's such a classic that some recipes list "soffritto" simply as an ingredient with no other explanation. A basic soffritto usually consists of onion, garlic, green bell pepper and celery, sometimes with a little carrot or pancetta added. The finely chopped ingredients are sautéed slowly to soften and caramelize the flavors and are used in soups and sauces.

Making Quick Salsa Crudo

This is literally a "raw sauce" of vegetables or fruits, and it's easy to create your own combinations of flavor. A good basic start for a salsa crudo is chiles, peppers, onions, and garlic. Serve with grilled chicken, pork, lamb or fish.

1 Peel, deseed or trim the vegetables as necessary, then use a sharp knife to cut into small, even dice. Try to combine texture and color as well as taste, and use chiles and other very spicy ingredients sparingly. Put all the diced ingredients into a bowl.

2 Add 1–2 tablespoons olive oil and a squeeze of lime or lemon juice and stir in finely chopped fresh basil, cilantro, flat-leaf parsley or mint, to enrich the flavor. Season to taste and toss well before serving.

To Peel Tomatoes

1 Cut a small cross in the skins of the tomatoes. Bring a pan of water to a boil and add the tomatoes. Turn off the heat and leave for 30 seconds, then lift out carefully with a draining spoon and place in a bowl of cold water. Using a small knife, peel off the skins.

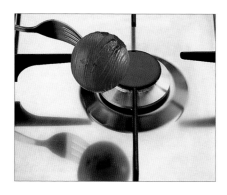

2 Alternatively, place the tomato firmly on the prongs of a fork and hold in a gas flame until the skin blisters and splits. When the tomatoes are cool enough to handle, peel off the skins using a small knife.

Grilling Vegetables for Purées and Sauces

Many puréed sauces or salsas call for cooked or grilled vegetables. Grilling is the best way to get the finest flavor from many vegetables, such as bell peppers, eggplant, tomatoes, garlic or onions, retaining and caramelizing the flavorful juices and tenderizing the flesh. However, since this method is not always practical, the next best is to roast the vegetables on a baking sheet under the broiler.

Roasted Vegetable Sauce

Serve roasted vegetable sauce with pork, ham, poultry or game. If you prefer a sauce with more texture, simply process for a shorter time.

Makes about 1¼ cups

INGREDIENTS

2 red or orange bell peppers
1 small onion
1 small eggplant
2 tomatoes with skins removed
2 garlic cloves, unpeeled
2–3 tablespoons olive oil
1 tablespoon lemon juice
½ cup fresh white bread crumbs

1 Cut the peppers, onion and eggplant in half, leaving the skins on, and, if necessary, remove any seeds and core. Place the vegetables cut-side down on a baking sheet with the garlic cloves. Place under a very hot broiler, or in a hot oven and cook until the skins are blackened and charred, and the flesh is tender.

2 Remove from heat and leave until cool enough to handle, then peel off the skins from the peppers and onions.

3 Scoop the flesh from the eggplant, and squeeze the flesh from the garlic.

4 Place all the vegetables in a blender or food processor and process to a very smooth purée, adding oil and lemon juice to taste. If you prefer a very smooth sauce, rub the purée through a fine sieve.

5 To thicken a vegetable puree, stir in a handful of fresh bread crumbs and process for a few seconds to the desired consistency.

Savory Butter Sauces

The simplest sauce of all is a melted butter sauce, flavored with lemon juice or herbs—ideal to drizzle on a simply cooked piece of fish or vegetables. A more refined version of this is clarified butter sauce, which is butter with the moisture and impurities removed.

Emulsions of butter with vinegar or other flavorings make deliciously rich beurre blanc or hollandaise sauce. Cold, flavored butters are useful to add last-minute melting flavors onto hot foods, and can be shaped prettily for extra garnish.

Blender Hollandaise

Hollandaise is a wonderfully rich butter sauce, much like a hot mayonnaise. This quick method eliminates whisking by hand and uses a blender to incorporate the ingredients to a thick, smooth emulsion where two liquids are combined by the dispersion of one in the other.

Makes 1 cup

INGREDIENTS

4 tablespoons white wine vinegar
6 peppercorns
1 bay leaf
3 egg yolks
¾ cup clarified butter
salt and ground black pepper

1 Place the wine vinegar, peppercorns and bay leaf in a small pan and heat until boiling, then simmer to reduce to about 1 tablespoon. Remove from heat and discard the flavorings.

2 Place the egg yolks in the blender and start the motor. Add the reduced white wine vinegar liquid through the feeder tube and blend for 10 seconds.

3 Heat the butter until hot. With the motor running, pour the butter through the feeder tube in a thin, steady stream until thick and smooth. Adjust the seasoning to taste with salt and pepper, and serve warm with poached fish, eggs or vegetables.

PREVENTING CURDLING

If hollandaise sauce is overheated, or if the butter is added too quickly, it may curdle and become slightly granular in texture. If this happens, remove it from heat immediately, before the sauce separates.

Quickly drop an ice cube into the sauce, then beat hard until the cube melts and cools the sauce. It also helps to stand the pan in a bowl of ice water while whisking in the ice cube.

Beurre Blanc

Vinaigre + beurre

This is one of the simplest sauces to make. White wine and vinegar are reduced in volume over high heat to produce an intense flavor. Butter is whisked into the liquid to enrich and thicken it. It is good with poached or grilled fish or chicken.

1 Place 3 tablespoons each of white wine vinegar and dry white wine in a small saucepan with a finely chopped shallot. Bring to a boil and boil until reduced to about 1 tablespoon.

2 Cut 1 cup chilled unsalted butter into small cubes. Over low heat, gradually whisk in the butter, piece by piece, letting each piece melt and be absorbed before adding the next. Season to taste and serve immediately.

How to Clarify Butter

Ideal for serving with vegetables such as asparagus or artichokes, clarified butter is butter that has been melted and has had all the salts, moisture and impurities removed, leaving it clear, with a rich, pure flavor. Clarified butter, called ghee in Indian cooking, keeps longer and can be heated to higher temperatures than ordinary butter without the risk of burning. It can be used for sautéing, and in sauces it gives a mild flavor and a high gloss. There are two main methods of clarifying:

Place the butter in a saucepan with an equal amount of water. Heat until the butter melts. Remove the pan from heat and let cool until the butter sets. Carefully lift out the fat, leaving the water and solids behind.

Alternatively, melt the butter in a small pan over very low heat, then skim off the froth with a perforated spoon. Pour the rest through a sieve lined with fine muslin, to strain out the solids.

Making Savory Butters

Flavored butters can be shaped or piped decoratively to serve with grilled steaks or poached or grilled fish.

To make an herb-flavored butter, finely chop your choice of fresh herbs. Beat the butter until softened, then stir in the herbs to mix evenly.

Making Shaped Slices

To make butter slices, chill lightly, roll the butter into a long sausage-shape and wrap in nonstick paper or plastic wrap. Chill and cut off slices of the butter as needed.

Piping Butter

Using a star nozzle, pipe softened butter onto nonstick baking parchment.

Making Shaped Butters

To make shaped butter pats, chill lightly, roll out the butter between two sheets of nonstick baking parchment. Chill until firm, then remove the top sheet and stamp out small shapes with a cutter.

Flavorings for Savory Butters

As well as being the traditional accompaniment to steaks, flavored butters can be rubbed onto meat before roasting or spread on chops and cutlets before grilling. They can also be spread on fish that is aluminum foil-wrapped and baked in the oven or used as you would garlic butter to make deliciously flavored breads.

• Finely chopped herbs, e.g. chives, parsley, dill, mint, thyme or rosemary. Use one herb or a combination of your choice, and add as much as the butter will comfortably absorb, or to achieve the desired flavor.

• Finely grated lemon, lime or orange zest and juice.

• Finely chopped canned anchovy fillets.

• Finely chopped gherkins or capers.

• Crushed, dried chiles or finely chopped fresh chiles.

• Crushed, fresh garlic cloves, or roasted garlic purée.

• Ground coriander seeds, curry spices or paste.

Savory Egg Sauces

The versatility of eggs comes in handy in all kinds of sauces, most commonly for thickening and enriching cooked sauces, or for holding an emulsion such as in mayonnaise. Keep spare egg yolks in the freezer, ready to enrich sauces whenever needed—stir in a pinch of salt or sugar before freezing to prevent them from thickening.

Mayonnaise

The texture of a hand-whisked mayonnaise is quite unlike any other —smooth, glossy and rich, the perfect partner to delicately poached salmon or a chicken salad. The choice of oil for mayonnaise depends on personal taste, but most people would find mayonnaise made with extra virgin olive oil too powerful in flavor. So, it's a good idea to use either pure olive oil, or alternatively a mix of half pure olive oil with half sunflower oil, or another lighter-flavored oil.

It is easier to get a good emulsion and prevent the mayonnaise from curdling if all the ingredients are at room temperature.

Makes about 1¼ cups

INGREDIENTS

2 egg yolks
1 tablespoon lemon juice
1 teaspoon Dijon mustard
1¼ cups light olive oil
salt and ground black pepper

1 Place the egg yolks, lemon juice, mustard, salt and pepper in a bowl and beat the egg yolk mixture until smooth and evenly combined.

2 Pouring with one hand and whisking with the other, add the oil gradually, drop by drop, making sure that each drop is whisked in before adding more.

3 Once a thick emulsion has formed, the oil can be poured faster, in a fine, steady stream, whisking until the mixture becomes smooth and thick. Adjust the seasoning to taste.

Using a Food Processor for Mayonnaise

A food processor can speed up the making of mayonnaise. Use a whole egg instead of the egg yolks.

Process the egg and flavorings for a few seconds, then slowly pour in the oil through the feeder tube in a thin, steady stream with the motor running, until the mixture forms a smooth, creamy texture.

Preventing Mayonnaise from Separating

If the oil is added too quickly, the mayonnaise may separate, but this can be corrected if you work quickly.

Break a fresh egg yolk into a clean bowl. Gradually whisk in the separated mayonnaise, a small spoonful at a time, whisking constantly, until it begins to thicken. Continue until all the mixture has been incorporated.

MAYONNAISE VARIATIONS

• For Garlic Mayonnaise, crush 3–6 garlic cloves into the ingredients.
• For Spicy Mayonnaise, add in 1 tablespoon of mustard, ½–1 teaspoon Worcestershire sauce and a dash of Tabasco sauce.
• For Green Mayonnaise, combine 1 ounce each of parsley and watercress sprigs in a blender or food processor. Add 3–4 chopped spring onions and 1 garlic clove. Blend until finely chopped. Add 4fl oz/120ml mayonnaise and blend until smooth. Season to taste.
• For Blue Cheese Dressing, mix 8 ounces crumbled Danish blue cheese into the mayonnaise.

Sweet Egg Sauces

Sweet egg sauces include many rich and creamy techniques, from classic egg-based custards to serve with pudding to light and fluffy sabayon that can be served on its own or as a luxurious sauce for gilded fruits or traditional baked custard that can be served hot or cold.

Egg Custard Sauce

Crème anglaise is the traditional vanilla custard sauce made with eggs, a far cry from the quick powder versions so often used. As well as being served as a classic sauce, either hot or cold, *crème anglaise* is often used as the base for other sweet sauces, such as the *crème pâtissière* used to fill éclairs and profiteroles. It's frequently enriched with cream instead of milk, or flavored with liqueurs for special desserts.

The trick here is to be patient—the egg must be cooked slowly; if it's overheated it will turn into scrambled eggs.

Makes about 1⅔ cups

INGREDIENTS

1¼ cups milk
1 vanilla bean
3 egg yolks
1 tablespoon sugar

1 Heat the milk with the vanilla bean until just boiling, then remove from heat. (To intensify the flavor split the bean lengthwise.) Cover and let infuse for 10 minutes, then strain into a clean pan. Beat the eggs and sugar together lightly in a bowl.

2 Pour the milk onto the eggs, whisking constantly.

3 Pour into the pan and stir until the custard thickens just enough to lightly coat the back of a wooden spoon. Remove from heat and pour into a bowl to prevent overcooking.

Preventing Curdling

Remove the egg custard from heat and plunge the bottom of the pan into cold water. Whisk in a teaspoonful of cornstarch until smooth, then reheat.

Sabayon Sauce

1 Whisk 1 egg yolk and 1 tablespoon sugar per portion in a bowl over a pan of simmering water. Whisk in 2 tablespoons sweet white wine, liqueur or full-flavored fruit juice, for each egg yolk. Whisk the sauce over constant heat until frothy.

2 Whisk until the sauce holds a trail on top of the mixture. Serve immediately or whisk until cool.

Baked Custard

Preheat the oven to 350°F. Grease an ovenproof dish. Beat together 4 large eggs, a few drops of vanilla and 1–2 tablespoons sugar. Whisk in 2½ cups hot milk, then strain into the prepared dish. Stand the dish in a roasting pan and pour in warm water to half fill the pan. Bake for 50–60 minutes.

Dessert Sauces

As well as the popular custards and flavored white sauces, quick and easy dessert toppings can be made almost instantly from ready-made ingredients, and these are ideal to serve on scoops of ice cream. They could also be served with pancakes and are particularly popular with children.

How to Use Vanilla Beans

Vanilla beans are commonly used in sweet dessert sauces, but they are occasionally used to flavor delicate savory cream sauces.

To flavor sugar, bury a vanilla bean in a jar of sugar. It can be used as vanilla-flavored sugar to add to sweet sauces and desserts.

To infuse vanilla flavor into milk or cream, heat it gently with the vanilla bean over low heat until almost boiling. Remove from heat, cover and let stand for 10 minutes. Remove the bean, rinse and dry; it may be re-used several times in this way.

To get maximum flavor from the bean, use a sharp knife to slit the bean lengthwise and open out. Use the tip of the knife to scrape out the sticky black seeds inside and add to the hot sauce.

Speedy Sauces for Topping Ice Cream

Lots of staple ingredients can be quickly transformed into irresistible sauces to spoon on top of ice cream, so you'll always have a quick dessert.

Marshmallow Melt

Melt 3½ ounces marshmallows with 2 tablespoons milk or cream in a small pan. Add a little grated nutmeg and spoon onto ice cream.

Black Forest Sauce

Drain a can of black cherries, reserving the juice. Blend a little of the juice with a little arrowroot or cornstarch. Add the cornstarch mixture to the remaining juice in a saucepan. Stir over medium heat until boiling and lightly thickened, then add the cherries and a dash of kirsch. Bubble for a few seconds, then spoon onto the ice cream and top with grated chocolate.

Chocolate-toffee Sauce

Chop a Heath bar and heat very gently in a saucepan, stirring until just melted. Spoon onto scoops of vanilla ice cream and sprinkle with chopped nuts.

Marmalade Whisky Sauce

Heat 4 tablespoons chunky marmalade in a pan with 2 tablespoons whisky, until just melted. Let bubble for a few seconds then spoon over ice cream.

Whiskey Sauce

Measure 2½ cups milk. Mix together 2 tablespoons cornstarch with 1 tablespoon of the milk. Bring the remaining milk to a boil, remove from heat and pour a little on the cornstarch mixture. Return the mixture to the pan and heat gently, stirring constantly, until thickened. Simmer for 2 minutes.

Remove from heat and stir in 2 tablespoons sugar and 4–6 tablespoons whiskey, to taste.

Presentation Ideas

When you've made a delicious sauce for a special dessert, why not make more of it by using it for decoration on the plate, too? Try one of the following simple ideas to make your sauce into a talking point. Individual slices of desserts, cakes or tarts, or a stuffed baked peach, look especially good like this.

Marbling

Use this technique when you have two contrasting sauces of similar thickness, such as a fruit purée with custard or cream. Spoon alternate spoonfuls of the sauces into a bowl or onto a serving plate, then stir the two sauces lightly together, swirling to create a marbled effect.

Yin-Yang Sauces

This is ideal for two contrasting colors of purée or coulis, such as a raspberry and a mango fruit coulis. Spoon one sauce on each side of a serving plate and push them together gently with a spoon, swirling one around the other, to make a yin-yang shape.

Drizzling

Pour a smooth sauce or coulis into a pitcher with a fine pouring lip. Drizzle the sauce in droplets or a fine wavy line onto the plate around the food.

Piping Outlines

Spoon a small amount of fruit coulis or chocolate sauce into a piping bag fitted with a plain writing nozzle. Pipe the outline of a shape onto a serving plate, then spoon in sauce to fill the inside.

Feathering Hearts

Flood the plate with a smooth sauce such as fruit purée. Add small droplets of cream into it at intervals. Draw the tip of a small knife through the cream, to drag each drop into a heart.

Quick Sauces for Crêpes

Rich Butterscotch Sauce

Heat 6 tablespoons butter, 1½ cups brown sugar and 2 tablespoons golden syrup or light corn syrup in a pan over low heat until melted. Remove from heat and add 5 tablespoons heavy cream, stirring continuously, until smooth. If desired, add about ½ cup chopped walnuts. Serve hot with ice cream and crêpes or waffles.

Orange Sauce

Melt 2 tablespoons unsalted butter in a heavy saucepan. Stir in ¼ cup sugar and cook until golden brown. Add the juice of 2 oranges and ½ lemon and stir until the caramel has dissolved.

Summer Berries

Melt 2 tablespoons of butter in a frying pan. Add in ¼ cup sugar and cook until golden brown. Add the juice of 2 oranges and cook until syrupy. Add 3 cups mixed berries and warm through. Add 3 tablespoons of Grand Marnier and set on fire. Spoon onto the crêpes.

Fruit Sauces

From the simplest fresh fruit purée, to cooked and thickened fruit sauces, there are hundreds of ways to add flavor to puddings, tarts and pies. The addition of a little liqueur or lemon juice can bring out the fruit flavor and prevent discoloration. Some fruit sauces, notably apple and cranberry, go well with meat and poultry dishes, and fresh fruit salsas can be eaten to cool down spicy hot dishes.

Making a Fruit Coulis

A delicious fruit coulis will add a sophisticated splash of color and flavor to desserts and ices. It can be made from either fresh or frozen fruit, in any season. Berries such as raspberries, black currants or strawberries are ideal, and tropical fruits like mango and kiwi fruit can be quickly transformed into exotically flavored coulis. A few drops of orange flower water or rose water will give a scented flavor, but use with caution—too much will overpower delicate ingredients.

Remove any hulls, stems, peel or pits from the fruit.

2 Place the prepared fruit in a blender or food processor and process until smooth.

3 Press the purée through a fine sieve, to remove the pips or fibrous parts and leave a smooth, syrupy juice. Sweeten to taste with confectioners' sugar and, if necessary, add a squeeze of lemon juice to sharpen the flavor.

COOK'S TIP

For cooked peeled fruit, mash with a potato masher for a coarser purée.

Peach Sauce

Purée a 14-ounce can of peaches, together with their juice and ¼ teaspoon of almond extract in a blender or food processor; chill before serving with fruit tarts or cakes.

Passion Fruit Coulis

Cut 3 ripe papayas in half and scoop out the seeds. Peel them and cut the flesh into chunks. Thread the chunks on bamboo skewers.

Halve eight passion fruit and scoop out the flesh. Purée in a blender for a few seconds.

2 Press the pulp through a sieve and discard the seeds. Add 2 tablespoons of lime juice, 2 tablespoons of confectioners' sugar and 2 tablespoons of white rum. Stir well until the sugar has dissolved.

3 Spoon some of the coulis onto a serving plate. Place the skewers on top. Drizzle the remaining coulis on the skewers and garnish with a little toasted coconut, if desired.

Chocolate Sauces

Chocolate sauces are enduringly popular, from simple custards to richly indulgent versions combined with liqueur or cream. They can be served with ice cream and other frozen desserts, but are also delicious with poached pears and a wide range of desserts. Flavored liqueurs can be chosen to echo the flavor of the dessert, and coffee, brandy and cinnamon all go especially well with chocolate.

The more cocoa solids chocolate contains, the more chocolatey the flavor will be. Semi-sweet chocolate may have between 30–70 percent of cocoa solids. Dark chocolate has around 75 percent, so if you're aiming for a really rich, dark sauce, this is the best choice. Milk chocolate is much sweeter, containing 20 percent cocoa solids.

White chocolate contains no cocoa solids, so strictly speaking it is not a chocolate at all, but gets its flavor from cocoa butter.

The best method of melting chocolate is in a double boiler or in a bowl over a pan of hot water. Never let water or steam come into contact with the chocolate, as this may cause it to stiffen. Overheating will also spoil the flavor and texture. Semi-sweet chocolate should not be heated above 120°F, and milk or white chocolate not above 110°F.

For sauce recipes where the chocolate is melted with a liquid such as milk or cream, the chocolate may be melted with the liquid in a pan over direct heat, providing there is plenty of liquid. Heat gently, stirring until melted.

Cocoa powder is ground from the whole cocoa mass after most of the cocoa butter has been extracted.

Creamy Chocolate Sauce

Place ½ cup heavy cream in a saucepan and add 4½ ounces chocolate pieces to the pan. Stir over low heat until the chocolate has melted. Serve warm or cold.

COOK'S TIP

If you run out of chocolate for a sauce recipe, you can use cocoa powder as an emergency substitute. Mix 3 tablespoons cocoa powder with 1 tablespoon melted butter to replace each 1 ounce chocolate.

Chocolate Custard Sauce

1 Melt 3½ ounces plain dark chocolate in a bowl over a pan of hot water.

2 Heat a scant 1 cup *crème anglaise* until hot but not boiling and stir in the melted chocolate until evenly mixed. Serve hot or cold.

Rich Chocolate Brandy Sauce

Break up 4 ounces semi-sweet chocolate into a bowl over a pan of hot water, then heat gently until melted. Remove from heat and add 2 tablespoons brandy and 2 tablespoons melted butter, then stir until smooth. Serve hot.

Making Marinades and Dressings

Marinades can be savory or sweet, spicy, fruity, fragrant or exotic, to add a contrasting flavor to all kinds of foods. They're useful not only for adding flavor but also for tenderizing and keeping foods moist during cooking, and can also be used to form the basis of a sauce to serve with the finished dish.

Oil-based Marinades

Choose an oil-based marinade for low-fat foods, such as lean meat, poultry or white fish, which may dry out during cooking. Oil-based marinades are especially useful for grilling and at their simplest consist of oil with crushed garlic and chopped herbs. Add crushed chiles for a hot and spicy marinade. Avoid adding salt to a marinade, as this draws the juices out of the meat.

| Place the marinade ingredients in a measuring cup and beat well with a fork to mix thoroughly. Arrange the food in a single layer in a non-metallic dish and pour on the marinade.

2 Turn the food to coat evenly in the marinade. Cover and leave in the refrigerator to marinate from 30 minutes to several hours, depending on the recipe. Turn the food occasionally.

3 When ready to cook, remove the food from the marinade. The marinade can be poured into a small pan and simmered for several minutes until thoroughly heated, then served spooned onto the cooked food.

Wine- or Vinegar-based Marinades

Wine- or vinegar-based mixtures are best with rich foods such as game or oily fish, to add flavor and to contrast with and balance richness. Use herb-flavored vinegars for oily fish and add chopped fresh herbs, such as tarragon, parsley, cilantro and thyme.

The acid in the wine or vinegar starts the tenderizing process well before cooking. For game, which can have a tendency to be tough, leave in the marinade overnight. Add lemon juice, garlic, black pepper and herbs, and even sherry, cider or orange juice according to your preference.

Yogurt is a good marinade and can be flavored with crushed garlic, lemon juice, and handfuls of chopped mint, thyme or rosemary for grilled lamb or pork. For fish or shellfish, use a marinade based on lemon juice with a little oil and plenty of black pepper.

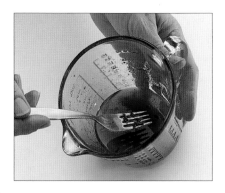

| Measure the ingredients into a bowl and beat with a fork.

2 Arrange the food in a wide, non-metallic dish in a single layer and spoon on the marinade, turning the food to coat evenly. Cover with plastic wrap and chill for 30 minutes up to several hours, depending on the recipe.

3 Drain the food of excess marinade before cooking. If the food is to be griddled or grilled, use the marinade to brush onto the food during cooking to add extra flavor and keep it moist.

Making an Oil-based Dressing

A good vinaigrette can do more than dress a salad. It can also be used to baste meat, poultry, seafood or vegetables during cooking. Many classic dressings, such as vinaigrette or French dressing, are based on an oil and acid mixture. The basic proportions are 3 parts oil to 1 part acid beaten together to form an emulsion. This can be done by simply whisking with a fork in a jug, or the ingredients can be placed in a screw-topped jar and shaken thoroughly. The oil you choose for a dressing adds character to the flavor, and which one you use for which dressing depends upon your own taste and upon the salad ingredients. A strongly flavored extra virgin olive oil adds personality to a simple green leaf or potato salad, but can overpower more delicate ingredients. Pure olive oil or sunflower oil adds a lighter flavor. Nut oils, such as walnut or hazelnut, are expensive, but can add a distinctive unusual flavor to a salad when used in small quantities.

The acid in a dressing may be vinegar or lemon juice, and this

VARIATIONS

- *Use red or white wine vinegar, or use a herb-flavored vinegar.*
- *Use lemon juice instead of vinegar.*
- *Replace 1 tablespoon of the vinegar with wine.*
- *Use olive oil, or a mixture of vegetable and olive oils.*
- *Use 4 fluid ounces olive oil and 2 tablespoons walnut or hazelnut oil.*
- *Add 1–2 tablespoons Dijon mustard to the vinegar before whisking in the oil.*
- *Add 1 crushed garlic clove before whisking in the oil.*
- *Add 1–2 tablespoons chopped herbs (parsley, basil, chives, thyme, etc) to the vinaigrette.*

can define the flavor of the finished salad. Choose from wine, sherry or cider vinegars, herb, chilli or fruit vinegars, to balance or contrast with the salad ingredients and the type of oil. Matured vinegars such as balsamic can be strong in flavor. Balsamic has a distinctive flavor, because of its ageing in wooden barrels and so the basic proportions of 3 parts oil to 1 of vinegar should be amended to 5 parts oil and 2 of balsamic vinegar.

Lemon juice adds a sharper flavor, which can be useful to add a lively tang to a bland dish. Other fruit juices, such as orange or apple juice can be used instead for a sweeter, less acid flavor.

Left: Bottled dressings make pleasing kitchen ornaments and excellent gift ideas.

Classic Vinaigrette

To ensure the ingredients blend together in a smooth emulsion, make sure all the ingredients are at room temperature.

Put 2 tablespoons vinegar in a bowl with 2 teaspoons Dijon mustard, salt and ground black pepper. Add ¼ teaspoon caster sugar if you like. Whisk to combine.

Slowly drizzle in 6 tablespoons oil, whisking constantly, until the vinaigrette is smooth and well blended. Check the seasoning and adjust if necessary.

Creamy Orange Dressing

This tangy orange dressing is versatile enough to complement a mixed green salad with orange segments and tomatoes. It could also partner grilled chicken or smoked duck breasts, or chicken kebabs, served on a bed of rice salad.

Serves 4

3 tablespoons half-fat crème fraîche
1 tablespoon white wine vinegar
finely grated rind and juice of 1 small orange
salt and ground black pepper

1 Measure the crème fraîche and wine vinegar into a screw-topped jar with the orange rind and juice.

2 Shake well until evenly combined, then adjust the seasoning to taste as desired.

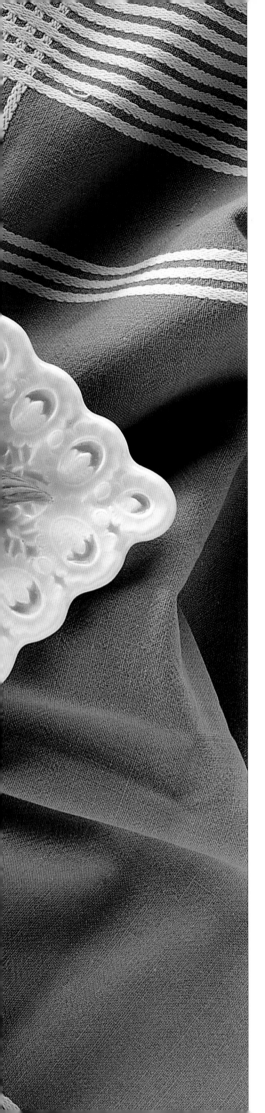

Classic Sauces

A comprehensive collection of sauce recipes must, by definition, include as its foundation the traditional, classic recipes that have been handed down through many generations of cooks.

Every country has its enduring time-honored sauces, from French favorites, such as elegant Béchamel Sauce, and rich, brown Espagnole Sauce, to British favorites such as Horseradish and Bread Sauce, all-American Cranberry Sauce to vibrant fresh Italian Pesto. Each has evolved from the imaginative use of local foods and has been created to enhance the flavors of the traditional cuisine of the country.

These classics form the basis of a repertoire essential to every professional cook. They encompass all of the sauce-making techniques, such as flour-thickened roux and rich emulsions, and some of them form an integral part of world-famous dishes.

In the past, the art of sauce-making required that stocks and other ingredients were prepared entirely by hand, but cooks today have electric mixers and food processors to assist them. The substitution of commercial stock can also save time and effort, and still provide the busy cook with impressive results, complementing the flavor of all kinds of dishes.

Béchamel Sauce

THIS IS A CREAMY white sauce with an excellent, mellow flavor, which makes it ideal for lasagne as well as a suitable base or accompaniment for many fish, egg and vegetable dishes.

Serves 4

INGREDIENTS

1 small onion

1 small carrot

1 celery stick

bouquet garni

6 black peppercorns

*pinch of freshly grated nutmeg or
    a blade of mace*

1¼ cups milk

2 tablespoons butter

¼ cup all-purpose flour

2 tablespoons light cream

salt and ground black pepper

1 Peel and finely chop the vegetables. Put the vegetables, flavorings and milk in a saucepan. Bring to a boil. Remove from heat, cover and let infuse for 30 minutes.

2 Over low heat, melt the butter in a saucepan, remove from heat and stir in the flour. Return to the heat and cook for 1–2 minutes, stirring, to make a roux.

3 Reheat the flavored milk until almost boiling. Strain into a bowl, pressing the vegetables with the back of a spoon to extract the juices.

4 Off the heat, gradually blend the milk into the roux, stirring vigorously after each addition. Bring to a boil and stir continuously until the sauce thickens. Simmer gently for 3–4 minutes.

5 Remove the pan from heat. Season with salt and pepper to taste and stir in the cream.

Basic White Sauce

THIS WHITE SAUCE IS wonderfully adaptable for all kinds of savory dishes, but it can be bland so always taste and season carefully.

Serves 6

INGREDIENTS

2½ cups milk
2 tablespoons butter
¼ cup all-purpose flour
salt and ground black pepper

1 Warm the milk in a saucepan over low heat, but do not boil.

2 In a separate saucepan melt the butter, then stir in the flour and cook gently for 1–2 minutes to make a roux. Do not let the roux brown.

3 Remove the pan from heat, gradually blend in the milk, stirring vigorously after each addition to prevent lumps from forming.

4 Return to the heat and bring to a boil slowly, stirring continuously until the sauce thickens.

5 Simmer gently for another 3–4 minutes, until thickened and smooth. Season with salt and ground black pepper to taste.

COOK'S TIPS

• For a thicker, coating sauce, increase the amount of flour to ½ cup and the butter to ¼ cup.
• If you aren't using a nonstick pan, use a small whisk to incorporate the flour and milk smoothly.

VARIATIONS

• Parsley sauce is traditionally served with bacon, fish and fava beans. Stir in 2 tablespoons chopped fresh parsley just before serving.
• Cheese sauce makes delicious egg and vegetable gratins. Stir in ½ cup finely grated aged Cheddar and ½ teaspoon prepared mustard.

Velouté Sauce

THIS SAVORY POURING SAUCE is named after its smooth, velvety texture. It's based on a white stock made from fish, vegetables or meat, so it can easily be adapted to the dish you are serving.

Serves 4

INGREDIENTS

2½ cups stock
2 tablespoons butter
¼ cup all-purpose flour
2 tablespoons light cream
salt and ground black pepper

1 Heat the stock until almost boiling, but do not boil. In another pan melt the butter and stir in the flour. Cook, stirring, over medium heat for 3–4 minutes or until a pale, straw color, stirring continuously.

2 Remove the pan from heat and gradually blend in the hot stock. Return to the heat and bring to a boil, stirring continuously, until the sauce thickens.

3 Continue to cook at a very slow simmer, stirring occasionally, until reduced by about a quarter.

4 Skim the surface during cooking to remove any scum, or pour through a very fine strainer.

5 Just before serving, remove from heat and stir in the cream. Season to taste.

VARIATION

For a richer flavor in a special dish, replace 2–3 tablespoons of the stock with dry white wine or vermouth.

Lemon Sauce with Tarragon

THE SHARPNESS OF LEMON and the mild aniseed flavor of tarragon add zest to chicken, egg or steamed vegetable dishes.

Serves 4

INGREDIENTS

1 lemon
a small bunch of fresh tarragon
1 shallot, finely chopped
6 tablespoons white wine
1 batch Velouté sauce
3 tablespoons heavy cream
2 tablespoons brandy
salt and ground black pepper

1 Thinly pare the zest from the lemon, taking care not to remove any white pith. Squeeze the juice from the lemon and pour it into a saucepan. Discard the lemon.

2 Discard the coarse stems from the tarragon. Chop the leaves and add all but 1 tablespoon to the pan with the lemon zest and shallot.

3 Add the wine and simmer gently until the liquid is reduced by half. Strain into a clean saucepan.

4 Add the Velouté sauce, cream, brandy and reserved tarragon. Heat through, taste and adjust the seasoning if necessary.

COOK'S TIP

This sauce goes well with pieces of boned chicken breast, wrapped with bacon and grilled or pan-fried.

Espagnole Sauce

ESPAGNOLE IS A CLASSIC rich brown sauce, ideal for serving with red meat and game. It also makes a delicious, full-flavored base for other sauces.

Serves 4–6

INGREDIENTS

2 tablespoons butter
2 ounces bacon, chopped
2 shallots, unpeeled and chopped
1 carrot, chopped
1 celery stalk, chopped
mushroom trimmings (if available)
¼ cup all-purpose flour
2½ cups hot brown stock
bouquet garni
2 tablespoons tomato paste
1 tablespoon sherry (optional)
salt and ground black pepper

1 Melt the butter in a heavy saucepan and fry the bacon for 2–3 minutes. Add the shallots, carrot, celery and mushroom trimmings, if using, and cook the mixture for another 5–6 minutes or until golden.

2 Gradually stir in the flour and cook for 5–10 minutes over medium heat, until the roux has become a rich brown color.

3 Remove the pan from heat and gradually blend in the stock.

4 Slowly bring to a boil, continuing to stir until the sauce thickens. Add the bouquet garni, tomato paste, sherry, if using, and seasoning. Reduce the heat and simmer gently for one hour, stirring occasionally.

5 Strain the Espagnole sauce, and gently reheat before serving.

COOK'S TIP

This sauce can be covered and stored in the refrigerator for up to 4 days, or it can be frozen for up to 1 month. It's worth making a double batch and keeping a batch in reserve.

Chasseur Sauce

THIS EXCELLENT MUSHROOM and
wine sauce will transform simple
pan-fried or grilled chicken, grilled
or roast pork, or rabbit dishes. To
give the sauce more flavor use
chestnut mushrooms.

Serves 3–4

INGREDIENTS

2 tablespoons butter
1 shallot, finely chopped
2 cups mushrooms, sliced
½ cup white wine
2 tablespoons brandy
1 batch Espagnole sauce
1 tablespoon chopped fresh tarragon
  or chervil

1 Melt the butter in a medium or large
saucepan over medium heat. Sauté
the shallot until soft but not brown.

2 Add the mushrooms and sauté,
stirring occasionally until they just
begin to brown.

3 Pour in the wine and brandy, and
simmer over medium heat until
reduced by half.

4 Add the Espagnole sauce and
herbs and heat through, stirring
occasionally. Serve hot.

Tangy Orange Sauce

KNOWN AS *SAUCE BIGARADE*, this is the perfect accompaniment for roast duckling and rich game. For a full mellow flavor it is best made with the rich roasting-pan juices.

Serves 4–6

INGREDIENTS

roasting-pan juices or
   2 tablespoons butter
⅓ cup all-purpose flour
½ pint hot stock (preferably duck)
⅔ cup red wine
2 Seville oranges or 2 sweet oranges plus
   2 teaspoons lemon juice
1 tablespoon orange-flavored liqueur
2 tablespoons red currant jelly
salt and ground black pepper

1 Carefully pour off any excess fat from the roasting pan, leaving the rich meat juices behind, or melt the butter in a small saucepan.

2 Sprinkle the flour into the juices or butter and cook, stirring continuously, for about 4 minutes, or until the mixture is lightly browned.

3 Off the heat, gradually blend in the hot stock and wine. Return to the heat and bring to a boil, stirring continuously. Lower the heat and simmer gently for 5 minutes.

4 Meanwhile, using a citrus zester, peel the zest thinly from one orange. Squeeze the juice from both of the oranges.

5 Place the zest in a small pan, cover with boiling water and bring back to a boil. Simmer for 5 minutes, then strain and add the zest to the sauce.

6 Add the orange juice to the sauce, along with the lemon juice, if using, and the liqueur and jelly. Stir until the jelly has dissolved. Season with salt and pepper to taste.

COOK'S TIP

Seville oranges have a distinctive bitter flavor, which is good for savory dishes, but they have a short season. They can be frozen whole, or you can freeze the juice and zest separately.

Hollandaise Sauce

A RICH BUTTER SAUCE much like a warm mayonnaise, is perfect for either steamed or grilled fish, such as salmon, or fresh vegetables such as broccoli, asparagus or new potatoes. The secret of success is patience. Slowly and thoroughly work in the butter to give a thick, glossy texture.

Serves 2–3

INGREDIENTS

2 tablespoons white wine or tarragon vinegar

1 tablespoon water

6 black peppercorns

1 bay leaf

½ cup butter

2 egg yolks

salt and ground black pepper

1 Place the vinegar, water, peppercorns, and bay leaf in a saucepan. Simmer the liquid gently until it has reduced by half. Strain and let cool.

2 In a separate bowl, cream the butter until soft.

3 In a double boiler, or a heatproof bowl sitting over a saucepan of gently simmering, but not boiling, water, whisk the egg yolks and infused vinegar liquid together gently until the mixture is light and fluffy.

4 Gradually add the butter a tiny piece at a time—about the size of a hazelnut will be enough. Whisk quickly until all the butter has been absorbed before adding any more.

5 Season lightly and, if the sauce is too sharp, add a little more butter.

6 For a thinner version of the sauce, stir in 1–2 tablespoons light cream. Serve immediately.

COOK'S TIP

Any leftover sauce can be stored in the refrigerator for up to a week. Reheat very gently in a bowl over simmering water, whisking continuously.

Mousseline Sauce

A TRULY LUSCIOUS SAUCE that is subtly flavored, rich and creamy. Try serving it as a dip for prepared artichokes or artichoke hearts, or with shellfish.

Serves 4

INGREDIENTS

2 egg yolks

1 tablespoon lemon juice

6 tablespoons softened butter

6 tablespoons heavy cream

extra lemon juice (optional)

salt and ground black pepper

1 To make the sauce, whisk the yolks and lemon juice in a bowl over a pan of barely simmering water, or a double boiler, until very thick and fluffy.

2 Whisk in the butter, but only a very little at a time, until it is thoroughly absorbed and the sauce has the consistency of mayonnaise.

3 In a separate bowl, whisk the cream until it forms stiff peaks. Fold into the warm sauce and adjust the seasoning. You can add a little more lemon juice for extra sharpness.

VARIATION

For a lavish accompaniment to special fish dishes such as lobster or Dover sole, stir in 2–3 tablespoons caviar before serving as a Caviar Mousseline.

Béarnaise Sauce

FOR DEDICATED MEAT EATERS, this
herbed butter sauce adds a note of
sophistication without swamping
your grilled or pan-fried steak. It
also enhances plain vegetables.

Serves 2–3

INGREDIENTS

3 tablespoons white wine vinegar

2 tablespoons water

1 small onion, finely chopped

a few fresh tarragon and chervil sprigs

1 bay leaf

6 crushed black peppercorns

½ cup butter

2 egg yolks

1 tablespoon chopped fresh herbs,
    such as tarragon, parsley, chervil

salt and ground black pepper

1 Place the vinegar, water, onion, herb
sprigs, bay leaf and peppercorns in a
saucepan. Simmer gently until the liquid
is reduced by half. Strain and cool.

2 In a separate bowl, cream the
butter until soft.

3 In a bowl over a saucepan of gently
simmering water, or a double
boiler, whisk the egg yolks and liquid
until light and fluffy.

4 Gradually add the butter, half a
teaspoonful at a time. Whisk until
all the butter has been incorporated
before adding any more.

5 Add the chopped fresh herbs and
season to taste.

6 Serve warm, not hot, on the side of
a steak or put a good spoonful on
new potatoes.

VARIATION

*To make Choron sauce, which is very
good with roast or grilled lamb, stir in
1 tablespoon tomato paste to the
sauce at the end of step 1.*

Newburg Sauce

THIS CREAMY MADEIRA-FLAVORED sauce originated in America. Its rich flavor will not mask delicate foods, and it is therefore ideal for serving with shellfish. It also goes well with pan-fried chicken.

Serves 4

INGREDIENTS

1 tablespoon butter
1 small shallot, finely chopped
pinch of cayenne pepper
1¼ cups heavy cream
4 tablespoons Madeira
3 egg yolks
salt and ground black pepper

1 Melt the butter in a heatproof bowl placed over a saucepan of simmering water, or in a double boiler.

2 Add the chopped shallot to the butter and cook gently until it is soft and transparent.

3 Add the cayenne and all but 4 tablespoons of the cream. Leave over the simmering water for 10 minutes to reduce slightly.

4 Stir in the Madeira. Beat the yolks with the remaining cream and stir into the hot sauce. Continue stirring the sauce over barely simmering water until thickened. Season to taste. Serve immediately.

COOK'S TIPS

• *To give the sauce a luxurious festive look, stir in 1–2 tablespoons of pink or black lumpfish roe at the end of cooking.*
• *Spoon onto seafood or chicken, reserving some for pouring, and serve immediately. Garnish the dish with fresh herbs.*

Pesto Sauce

THERE IS NOTHING MORE evocative of the warmth of Italy than a good homemade pesto. Serve stirred into your favorite pasta.

Serves 3–4

INGREDIENTS

1 cup basil leaves
2 garlic cloves, crushed
2 tablespoons pine nuts
½ cup olive oil
½ cup finely grated fresh
   Parmesan cheese
salt and ground black pepper

| **By hand:** Using a mortar and pestle, grind the basil, garlic, pine nuts and seasoning into a fine paste.

2 Transfer the mixture to a bowl and whisk in the oil a little at a time.

3 Add the cheese and blend well. Adjust the seasoning to taste and heat the sauce gently.

| **Using a food processor:** place the basil, garlic, pine nuts and seasoning in the food processor and process as finely as possible.

2 With the machine running slowly add the oil in a thin stream, combining the ingredients until they have formed a smooth paste.

3 Add the cheese and pulse quickly 3–4 times. Adjust the seasoning if necessary and heat gently.

VARIATION

Pesto makes an excellent dressing for boiled new potatoes. Serve while hot or let cool to room temperature.

Rich Tomato Sauce

FOR A FULL TOMATO flavor and rich red color, fresh Italian plum tomatoes are an excellent choice if they are available.

Serves 4–6

INGREDIENTS

2 tablespoons olive oil

1 large onion, chopped

2 garlic cloves, crushed

1 carrot, finely chopped

1 celery stalk, finely chopped

1½ pounds tomatoes, peeled and chopped

⅔ cup red wine

⅔ cup vegetable stock

bouquet garni

½–1 teaspoon sugar

1 tablespoon tomato paste, or to taste

salt and ground black pepper

1 Heat the oil in a saucepan, add the onion and garlic and sauté until soft and pale golden brown. Add the carrot and celery and continue to cook, stirring occasionally, until golden.

2 Stir in the tomatoes, wine, stock and bouquet garni. Season with salt and ground black pepper to taste.

3 Bring the tomato mixture to a boil, then cover and simmer gently for 45 minutes, stirring occasionally.

4 Remove the bouquet garni, taste the sauce and adjust the seasoning, adding sugar and tomato paste as necessary.

5 Serve the sauce as it is or, for a smoother texture, press through a sieve, or purée in a blender or food processor. This is delicious spooned over sliced zucchini or whole green beans.

Blue Cheese and Walnut Sauce

THIS IS A VERY quick but indulgently creamy sauce. The blue cheese melts easily with cream to make a simple sauce to serve with vegetables or pasta for a delicious lunch or supper.

Serves 2

INGREDIENTS

¼ cup butter

¾ cup button mushrooms, sliced

5 ounces hard blue cheese, such as Gorgonzola, Stilton or Danish Blue

⅔ cup sour cream

⅓ cup grated Pecorino cheese

⅓ cup broken walnut pieces

salt and ground black pepper

1 Melt the butter in a saucepan, add the mushrooms and gently sauté for 3–5 minutes, stirring occasionally, until lightly browned.

2 Place the blue cheese and cream in a bowl, add seasoning to taste, and mash together well using a fork.

3 Stir the cheese mixture into the mushroom mixture and heat gently, stirring, until melted.

4 Finally, stir in the Pecorino cheese and the walnut pieces. Serve warm.

Quick Saté Sauce

THERE ARE MANY VERSIONS of this tasty peanut sauce. This one is very easy and it tastes delicious drizzled over grilled or barbecued skewers of chicken. For parties, spear chunks of chicken with toothpicks and arrange around a bowl of warm sauce.

Serves 4

INGREDIENTS
scant 1 cup coconut cream
4 tablespoons crunchy peanut butter
1 teaspoon Worcestershire sauce
Tabasco sauce, to taste
fresh coconut, to garnish (optional)

1 Pour the coconut cream into a small saucepan and heat it gently over low heat for about 2 minutes.

2 Add the peanut butter and stir vigorously until it is blended into the coconut cream. Continue to heat until the mixture is warm but not boiling hot.

3 Add the Worcestershire sauce and a dash of Tabasco to taste. Pour into a serving bowl.

COOK'S TIP

Thick coconut milk can be substituted for coconut cream, but be sure to buy an unsweetened variety for this recipe.

4 Use a potato peeler to shave thin curls from a piece of fresh coconut, if using. Sprinkle the coconut on the dish of your choice and serve immediately with the sauce.

Green Peppercorn Sauce

THIS SAUCE IS EXCELLENT with pasta, pork steaks or grilled chicken. The green peppercorns in brine are a better choice than the dry-packed type because they tend to give a more rounded flavor.

Serves 3–4

INGREDIENTS

1 tablespoon green peppercorns in brine, drained
1 small onion, finely chopped
2 tablespoons butter
1¼ cups light stock
juice of ½ lemon
1 tablespoon beurre manié
3 tablespoons heavy cream
1 teaspoon Dijon mustard
salt and ground black pepper

1 Dry the peppercorns on absorbent paper towels, then crush lightly under the blade of a heavy-duty knife or use a mortar and pestle.

2 Soften the onion in the butter; add the stock and lemon juice and simmer for 15 minutes.

3 Whisk in the beurre manié a little at a time and continue to cook, stirring, until the sauce thickens.

VARIATION

For a lighter, less rich sauce, use crème fraîche instead of the heavy cream.

4 Reduce the heat and stir in the peppercorns, cream and mustard. Heat until boiling, then season to taste. Serve hot with buttered pasta or the dish of your choice.

COOK'S TIP

For beurre manié, mix together equal amounts of butter and flour.

Barbecue Sauce

BRUSH THIS SAUCE ON chops, kebabs or chicken drumsticks before cooking on the barbecue, or serve as a hot or cold accompaniment to hot dogs and burgers.

Serves 4

INGREDIENTS

2 tablespoons vegetable oil

1 large onion, chopped

2 garlic cloves, crushed

14-ounce can tomatoes

2 tablespoons Worcestershire sauce

1 tablespoon white wine vinegar

3 tablespoons honey

1 teaspoon mustard powder

½ teaspoon chili seasoning or mild chili powder

salt and ground black pepper

1 In a saucepan, heat the oil and sauté the onion and garlic until soft.

2 Stir in the remaining ingredients and bring to a boil. Simmer, uncovered, for 15–20 minutes, stirring occasionally. Cool slightly.

3 Pour into a food processor or blender and process until smooth.

4 Press the sauce through a sieve if you prefer smoother results, and adjust the seasoning with salt and pepper to taste before serving.

VARIATION

For a really rich, spicy chili flavor, omit the chili seasoning and add instead a small red chile, seeded and chopped. Leave the seeds in if you like it really hot.

Applesauce

REALLY MORE OF A condiment than a sauce, this tart purée is usually served cold or warm, rather than hot. It's typically served with rice, roast pork or duck, but is also good with cold meats and savory pies.

Serves 6

INGREDIENTS

8 ounces tart apples
2 tablespoons water
thin strip of lemon zest
1 tablespoon butter
1–2 tablespoons sugar

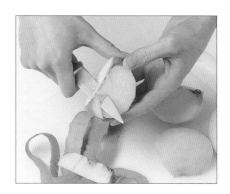

1 Peel the apples, cut into quarters and remove the core. Cut into thin, even slices.

2 Place the apples in a saucepan with the water and lemon zest. Cook, uncovered, over low heat, until very soft, stirring occasionally.

3 Remove the lemon zest from the pan and discard. Beat the apples into a pulp with a spoon, or press through a sieve.

4 Stir the butter into the applesauce and then add sugar to taste.

VARIATIONS

• To make a Normandy Apple Sauce, try stirring in 1 tablespoon Calvados with the butter and sugar at step 4.
• To make a creamy savory Applesauce, stir in 2 tablespoons sour cream or crème fraîche at step 4.

Mint Sauce

TART, YET SWEET, this simple sauce is the perfect foil to rich meat. It's best served, of course, with the new season's tender roast lamb, but it is also wonderful with grilled lamb chops or pan-fried duck.

Serves 6

INGREDIENTS

small bunch of mint
1 tablespoon sugar
2 tablespoons boiling water
3 tablespoons white wine vinegar

1 Strip the mint leaves from the stems and finely chop the leaves.

2 Place in a bowl with the sugar and pour on the boiling water. Stir well and let the mixture stand for 5–10 minutes.

3 Add the vinegar and let stand for 1–2 hours before serving.

COOK'S TIP

This sauce also makes a refreshing dressing to enhance the summery flavor of fresh peas or new potatoes.

Cranberry Sauce

THIS IS THE TRADITIONAL sauce for roast turkey, but don't keep it just for festive occasions. The vibrant color and tart taste are a perfect partner to any white roast meat, and it makes a great addition to a chicken or Brie sandwich.

Serves 6

INGREDIENTS

1 orange
2 cups cranberries
1¼ cups sugar
⅔ cup water

1 Pare the zest thinly from the orange using a swivel-bladed vegetable peeler, taking care not to remove any white pith. Squeeze the juice.

2 Place in a saucepan with the cranberries, sugar and water.

3 Bring to a boil, stirring until the sugar has dissolved, then let simmer gently for 10–15 minutes or until the berries burst.

4 Remove the orange zest and let cool before serving.

COOK'S TIP

Fresh or frozen cranberries may be used in this sauce, depending on the season. Use fresh as a first choice.

Horseradish Sauce

THIS LIGHT, CREAMY SAUCE has a peppery flavor that's spiced with just a hint of mustard. It is the classic accompaniment to roast beef, but is perfect, too, with herbed sausages and grilled fish, especially oily fish such as mackerel.

Serves 6

INGREDIENTS

3-inch piece fresh horseradish
1 tablespoon lemon juice
2 teaspoons sugar
½ teaspoon English mustard powder
⅔ cup heavy cream

1 Scrub and peel the piece of fresh horseradish, and then grate it as finely as possible.

2 In a bowl, mix the grated horseradish, lemon juice, sugar and mustard powder.

3 Whip the cream until it stands in soft peaks, then gently fold in the horseradish mixture.

VARIATION

For a change of flavor, replace the lemon juice with tarragon vinegar.

Bread Sauce

SMOOTH AND SURPRISINGLY DELICATE, this old-fashioned sauce dates back to medieval times. It's traditionally served with roast chicken, turkey and game birds.

Serves 6

INGREDIENTS

1 small onion
4 cloves
bay leaf
1¼ cups milk
scant 2 cups fresh
    white bread crumbs
1 tablespoon butter
1 tablespoon light cream
salt and ground black pepper

1 Peel the onion and stick the cloves into it. Put it into a saucepan with the bay leaf and pour in the milk.

2 Bring to a boil, then remove from heat and let infuse for 15–20 minutes. Remove the bay leaf and onion from the milk.

3 Return to the heat and stir in the bread crumbs. Simmer for 4–5 minutes or until thick and creamy.

4 Stir in the butter and cream, then season to taste.

COOK'S TIP

If you would prefer a less strong flavor, reduce the number of cloves in the onion to one or two and add a little freshly grated nutmeg to the milk instead.

Sauces for Pasta Dishes

There are hundreds of sauce recipes for all types of pasta, and not surprisingly they are often Italian in origin. Endlessly varied in style, they may be delicate, buttery herb mixtures or rich cream sauces, hearty meat ragús or chunky vegetable sauces. Many are based on tomatoes from southern Italy and make the very most of those other Mediterranean ingredients —olive oil, garlic and basil—all classic partners for pasta.

Most pasta sauces are refreshingly simple and foolproof, and do not need hours of preparation. Most are cooked in a matter of minutes, retaining all the natural flavors of fresh ingredients, with the exception of long-simmered rich meat and tomato ragús, which by tradition are simmered at length over a low flame for a more concentrated flavor.

Many of these sauces are designed to match particular types or shapes of pasta, but there are no hard and fast rules. Many of the sauces work well with other types of pasta, so try experimenting with your favorites.

It's rare for a pasta sauce to be flour-thickened, but many are enriched or thickened with eggs, such as Carbonara. Those that are simmered over long periods, such as Bolognese Sauce, reach a thicker consistency as they are reduced and become more concentrated. Many form an integral part of the dish and may be as simple as olive oil with Parmesan cheese and herbs. The choice is yours.

Making Pasta Dough

Homemade pasta has a wonderfully light, almost silky texture—quite different from the so-called fresh pasta that you buy at stores. If you use egg in the mixture, which is recommended if you are making pasta at home, the dough is easy to make, and the initial process is not that different from making bread.

Pasta with Eggs

INGREDIENTS

2¾ cups all-purpose flour
3 eggs
1 teaspoon salt

COOK'S TIP

Don't skimp on the kneading time, or the finished pasta will not be light and silky.

1 Mound the flour on a clean surface and make a large, deep well in the center with your hands. Keep the sides of the well so that when the eggs are added they will stay in the well.

2 Crack the eggs into the well and add the salt. With a table knife, mix the eggs and salt together, then gradually incorporate the flour from the sides of the well.

3 As soon as the mixture is no longer liquid, dip your fingers in the flour and work the ingredients into a rough and sticky dough. If the dough is too dry, add a few drops of cold water; if it is too moist, sprinkle a little flour over it.

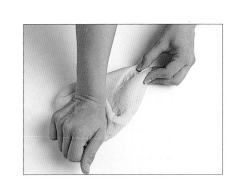

4 Press the dough into a rough ball and knead it as you would bread. Push it away from you with the heel of your hand, then fold the dough back on itself so that it faces toward you and push it out again.

5 Continue folding the dough back a little further each time and pushing it out until you have folded it back all the way toward you, and all the dough has been kneaded. Give the dough a quarter turn counter-clockwise, then continue kneading, folding and turning for 10 minutes. The dough should be very smooth and elastic.

6 Wrap the dough in plastic wrap and let it rest for 15–20 minutes at room temperature. It will then be ready to roll.

Making Pasta Shapes

1 Unwrap the dough and cut it in half. Work on half immediately.

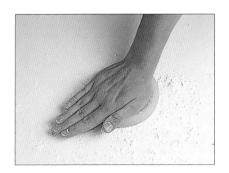

2 Sprinkle flour on the work surface, add the dough and flatten it.

3 Roll out the dough, turning it as you work until it is ⅛ inch thick.

Italian Plum Tomato Sauce with Cheese and Ham Ravioli

THIS TASTY SAUCE USES staple ingredients, which is time saving if you have an elaborate pasta to make. It can also be served with meat or fish.

Serves 4–6

INGREDIENTS

1¼ pounds fresh pasta dough with eggs

4 tablespoons grated fresh Pecorino cheese, plus extra to serve

For the filling

6 ounces ricotta cheese

2 tablespoons grated fresh Parmesan cheese

4 ounces prosciutto, finely chopped

5 ounces fresh mozzarella cheese, drained and finely chopped

1 small egg

1 tablespoon chopped fresh flat-leaf parsley, plus extra to garnish

For the Italian plum tomato sauce

2 tablespoons olive oil

1 onion, finely chopped

14-ounce can chopped plum tomatoes

1 tablespoon sun-dried tomato paste

1–2 teaspoons dried oregano

salt and ground black pepper

1 To make the sauce, heat the oil in a saucepan, add the onion and cook, stirring frequently, until softened.

2 Add the tomatoes. Fill the empty can with water, pour it into the pan, then stir in the tomato paste, oregano and seasoning to taste. Bring to a boil and stir well, then cover the pan and simmer for 30 minutes, stirring occasionally and adding more water if the sauce becomes too thick.

3 Put the filling ingredients in a bowl and season to taste. Mix with a fork, breaking up the ricotta.

4 Using a pasta machine, roll out one-quarter of the pasta into a 36–40-inch strip. Cut the strip into two 18–20-inch lengths.

5 Using two teaspoons, put little mounds of the filling, 10–12 in total, along one side of one of the pasta strips, spacing them evenly. The filling will be quite moist. Brush a little water around each mound, then fold over the plain side of the pasta strip.

6 Starting from the folded edge, press down gently with your fingertips around each mound, pushing the air out at the unfolded edge.

7 Sprinkle lightly with flour. With a fluted pasta wheel, cut along each long side, then in between each mound, to make small square shapes.

8 Put the ravioli on floured dish towels; sprinkle lightly with flour. Let dry while repeating the process with the remaining pasta, to give you 80–96 ravioli altogether.

9 Drop the ravioli into a large pan of boiling, lightly salted water, bring the water back to a boil and boil for 4–5 minutes. Drain well. Spoon about a third of the ravioli into a warmed serving bowl. Sprinkle with 1 tablespoon grated Pecorino and pour on a third of the tomato sauce.

10 Repeat the layers twice, then top with the remaining grated Pecorino. Serve immediately, garnished with chopped parsley.

Tomato and Chili Sauce with Pasta

THIS IS A SPECIALTY OF LAZIO in Italy
—the Italian name for the sauce,
al arrabbiata, means rabid or angry,
and describes the heat that comes
from the chile.

Serves 4

INGREDIENTS

11 ounces dried penne or tortiglioni

For the tomato and chile sauce

1¼ pounds sugocasa
2 garlic cloves, crushed
⅔ cup dry white wine
1 tablespoon sun-dried tomato paste
1 fresh red chile
2 tablespoons finely chopped parsley
salt and ground black pepper
grated fresh Pecorino cheese, to serve

1 Put the sugocasa, garlic, wine, tomato paste and whole chile in a saucepan and bring to a boil. Cover and simmer gently.

2 Drop the pasta into a large saucepan of rapidly boiling salted water and cook for 10–12 minutes or until *al dente*.

3 Remove the chile from the sauce and add the parsley. Taste for seasoning. If you prefer a hotter taste, chop some or all of the chile and return it to the sauce.

4 Drain the pasta and put into a warmed large bowl. Pour the sauce onto the pasta and toss to mix. Serve immediately, sprinkled with parsley and grated Pecorino.

COOK'S TIPS

• *If you prefer the flavor to be slightly less hot, remove the seeds from the chile before using. Split the chile down its length and scrape out the fiery seeds with the tip of a knife.*

• *Sugocasa literally means "house sauce" and consists of tomatoes, crushed coarsely so that they have a chunky texture.*

Sun-dried Tomato and Radicchio Sauce with Paglia e Fieno

THIS IS A LIGHT, MODERN pasta dish of the kind served in fashionable restaurants. It is the presentation that sets it apart. It is very quick and easy to prepare.

Serves 4

INGREDIENTS

3 tablespoons pine nuts
12 ounces paglia e fieno pasta
2 tablespoons extra virgin olive oil
4–6 scallions, thinly sliced into rings

**For the sun-dried tomato and
   radicchio sauce**
1 tablespoon extra virgin olive oil
2 tablespoons sun-dried tomato paste
1¹/₂ ounces radicchio leaves, finely shredded
salt and ground black pepper

1 Put the pine nuts in a heavy frying pan and toss over medium heat for 1–2 minutes, until they are lightly toasted and golden brown. Remove and set aside.

2 Cook the pasta according to the package instructions, keeping the colors separate by using two pans.

3 To make the sauce, heat 1 tablespoon of the oil in a medium frying pan or saucepan. Add the sun-dried tomato paste, then stir in two ladlefuls of pasta cooking water. Simmer until the sauce is slightly reduced, stirring constantly.

4 Stir in the shredded radicchio, then taste and season. Keep over a low heat. Drain the pasta, keeping the colors separate, and return them to the pans in which they were cooked. Add 1 tablespoon of oil to each pan and toss over medium to high heat until the pasta is glistening.

5 Arrange a portion of green and white pasta in each of four warmed bowls, then spoon the sun-dried tomato and radicchio sauce in the center. Sprinkle the scallions and toasted pine nuts decoratively on top and serve immediately. Before eating, each diner should toss the sauce with the pasta to mix well.

COOK'S TIP

If you find the presentation too fussy, you can toss the sun-dried tomato and radicchio mixture with the pasta in one large warmed bowl before serving, then sprinkle with scallions and pine nuts.

Cannelloni with Two Sauces

THE COMBINATION OF THE full-flavored tomato sauce and the creamy white sauce makes this cannelloni dish a success. For a special occasion, make it in advance to the baking stage. Add the white sauce and bake on the day.

Serves 6

INGREDIENTS

1 tablespoon olive oil
1 small onion, finely chopped
1 pound ground beef
1 garlic clove, finely chopped
1 teaspoon dried mixed herbs
½ cup beef stock
1 egg
*3 ounces cooked ham or Mortadella
    sausage, finely chopped*
*3 tablespoons fine fresh white
    bread crumbs*
1¼ cups freshly grated Parmesan cheese
18 precooked cannelloni tubes
salt and ground black pepper

For the tomato sauce

2 tablespoons olive oil
1 small onion, finely chopped
½ carrot, finely chopped
1 celery stalk, finely chopped
1 garlic clove, crushed
14-ounce can chopped plum tomatoes
a few sprigs of fresh basil
½ teaspoon dried oregano

For the white sauce

¼ cup butter
½ cup all-purpose flour
3¾ cups milk
fresh nutmeg

1 Heat the olive oil in a saucepan and cook the chopped onion over low heat, stirring occasionally, for about 5 minutes, until softened.

2 Add the ground beef and garlic and cook for 10 minutes, stirring and breaking up any lumps with a wooden spoon.

3 Add the herbs, and season to taste, then moisten with half the stock. Cover the pan and let simmer for 25 minutes, stirring occasionally and adding more stock as it reduces. Spoon into a bowl and let cool.

4 To make the tomato sauce, heat the olive oil in a saucepan, add the vegetables and garlic and cook over medium heat, stirring frequently, for 10 minutes. Add the tomatoes. Fill the empty can with water, pour it into the pan, then add the herbs, and season to taste. Bring to a boil, lower the heat, cover and simmer for 25–30 minutes, stirring occasionally. Purée the tomato sauce in a blender or food processor.

5 To the meat, add the egg, ham or mortadella, bread crumbs and 6 tablespoons of the grated Parmesan, and stir well to mix. Taste for seasoning.

6 Spread a little of the tomato sauce on the bottom of a rectangular baking dish. Using a teaspoon, fill the cannelloni with the meat mixture.

7 Place the cannelloni in a single layer on top of the sauce. Pour the remaining tomato sauce on top.

8 Preheat the oven to 375°F. For the white sauce, melt the butter in pan, add the flour and cook for 1–2 minutes. Remove from the heat and blend in the milk.

9 Return to the heat, bring to a boil and stir until smooth and thick. Grate in fresh nutmeg, and season.

10 Pour on the cannelloni, then sprinkle with Parmesan. Bake for 40–45 minutes. Let stand for 10 minutes before serving.

Tomato and Zucchini Sauce with Tagliatelle

THE TOMATO AND ZUCCHINI sauce goes well with a variety of pastas and only takes minutes to prepare.

Serves 3–4

INGREDIENTS

8 ounces whole-wheat tagliatelle

For the tomato and zucchini sauce

5–6 ripe plum tomatoes

2 tablespoons olive oil

1 onion, chopped

2 celery stalks, chopped

1 garlic clove, crushed

2 zucchini, halved lengthwise
  and sliced

2 tablespoons sun-dried tomato paste

salt and ground black pepper

To serve

½ cup sliced almonds, toasted

1 To make the sauce, place the tomatoes in a bowl of boiling water for 30 seconds to loosen the skins. Peel, then chop.

2 Bring a large pan of lightly salted water to a boil, add the pasta and cook for about 12 minutes, or according to the instructions on the package, until *al dente*.

3 Meanwhile, heat the oil in another pan and add the chopped onion, celery, garlic and zucchini.

4 Sauté over low heat for 3–4 minutes, until the onions have become lightly browned.

5 Stir in the tomatoes and sun-dried tomato paste. Cook gently for another 5 minutes, then add salt and pepper to taste.

6 Drain the pasta, return it to the pan and add the sauce. Toss well. Place in a serving dish and sprinkle the toasted almonds on top to serve.

COOK'S TIP

If using fresh pasta, you'll need a double batch, i.e. 1 pound tagliatelle for 3–4 hearty appetites. Fresh tagliatelle takes only 3–4 minutes to cook.

Carbonara Sauce with Spaghetti

AN ALL-TIME FAVORITE sauce that is perfect for spaghetti or tagliatelle. This version has plenty of pancetta or bacon and is not too creamy, but you can vary the amounts.

Serves 4

INGREDIENTS

12 ounces fresh or dried spaghetti

For the carbonara sauce

2 tablespoons olive oil

1 small onion, finely chopped

8 pancetta or lean bacon strips, cut into ¹/₂-inch strips

4 eggs

4 tablespoons crème fraîche

4 tablespoons freshly grated Parmesan cheese, plus extra to serve

salt and ground black pepper

1 Heat the oil in a frying pan, add the onion and cook, stirring, over low heat, for 5 minutes, until softened.

2 Add the strips of pancetta or bacon to the onion in the pan and cook for about 10 minutes, stirring almost constantly.

3 Meanwhile, cook the pasta in a pan of salted boiling water according to the instructions on the package, until *al dente*.

4 Put the eggs, crème fraîche and grated Parmesan in a bowl. Grind in plenty of pepper, then beat the mixture together well.

5 Drain the pasta, turn it into the pan with the pancetta or bacon and toss well to mix.

6 Turn the heat off under the pan. Immediately add the egg mixture and toss vigorously so that it cooks lightly and coats the pasta.

7 Quickly taste for seasoning, then divide among four warmed bowls and sprinkle with black pepper. Serve immediately, with extra grated Parmesan passed separately.

Gorgonzola Sauce with Gnocchi

THIS CHEESE SAUCE has a strong flavor and so is ideal with potato dumplings or a plain pasta like macaroni. Either way, it makes a filling dish ideal for a winter supper.

Serves 4

INGREDIENTS

1 pound potatoes, unpeeled
1 large egg
1 cup all-purpose flour
fresh thyme sprigs, to garnish
salt and ground black pepper
4 tablespoons freshly grated Parmesan
    cheese, to serve

For the Gorgonzola sauce

4 ounces Gorgonzola cheese
4 tablespoons heavy cream
1 tablespoon chopped fresh thyme

1 Cook the potatoes in boiling salted water for about 20 minutes, until they are tender. Drain and, when cool enough to handle, remove the skins.

2 Press the potatoes through a sieve, using the back of a spoon, into a mixing bowl. Season, then beat in the egg. Add the flour a little at a time, stirring well with a wooden spoon after each addition until you have a smooth dough. (You may not need all the flour.)

3 Turn the dough out onto a floured surface and knead it for about 3 minutes, adding more flour if you need to, until it is smooth and soft and not sticky to the touch.

4 Divide the dough into six equal pieces. Flour your hands and gently roll each piece on a board into a log shape measuring 6–8 inches long and 1 inch in diameter. Cut each log into six to eight pieces, each about 1 inch long, then gently roll each piece in the flour. Form into gnocchi by gently pressing each piece onto the floured surface with the tines of a fork to form ridges.

5 To cook, drop the gnocchi into a pan of boiling water about 12 at a time. Once they rise to the surface, after about 2 minutes, cook them for 4–5 more minutes, then drain.

6 To make the sauce, place the Gorgonzola, cream and thyme in a large frying pan and heat gently until the cheese melts to form a thick, creamy consistency, then heat through.

7 Add the drained gnocchi to the sauce and toss well to combine. Serve with Parmesan and garnish with thyme.

VARIATION

The Gorgonzola sauce could also be used in a fondue, with croutons or vegetable pieces to dip.

Cream and Parmesan Sauce with Spinach and Ricotta Ravioli

THIS CREAMY PARMESAN SAUCE is a perfect accompaniment to homemade spinach and ricotta ravioli but would be just as delicious on store-bought tortelloni or any other fresh pasta with a stuffing to give flavor.

Serves 8

INGREDIENTS

1¼ pounds fresh pasta dough
grated fresh Parmesan cheese, to serve

For the filling

3 tablespoons butter
6 ounces fresh spinach leaves, trimmed, washed and shredded
scant 1 cup ricotta cheese
⅓ cup freshly grated Parmesan cheese
freshly grated nutmeg
1 small egg
salt and ground black pepper

For the cream and Parmesan sauce

¼ cup butter
½ cup heavy cream
⅔ cup freshly grated Parmesan cheese

1 To make the filling, melt the butter in a saucepan, add the spinach and salt and pepper to taste and cook over medium heat for 5–8 minutes, stirring frequently, until the spinach is wilted and tender. Increase the heat to high. Stir until the water boils off and the spinach is quite dry.

2 Put the spinach in a bowl and set aside until cold, then add the ricotta, grated Parmesan and freshly grated nutmeg to taste. Beat well to mix, taste for seasoning, then add the egg and beat well again.

3 Using a pasta machine, roll out one-quarter of the pasta into a 36–40-inch strip. Cut the strip with a sharp knife into two 18–20-inch lengths (you can do this during rolling if the strip gets too long to manage).

4 Using a teaspoon, put 10–12 little mounds of the filling along one side of one of the pasta strips, spacing them evenly. Brush a little water around each mound, then fold the plain side of the pasta strip over the filling.

5 Starting from the folded edge, press down gently with your fingertips around each mound of filling, pushing the air out at the unfolded edge. Sprinkle lightly with flour.

6 With a fluted pasta wheel, cut along each long side, then in between each mound to make small square shapes.

7 Put the ravioli on floured dish towels, sprinkle lightly with flour and let dry while repeating the process with the remaining pasta, to give you 80–96 ravioli altogether.

8 Drop the ravioli into a large pan of boiling salted water, bring back to a boil and boil for 4–5 minutes.

9 Meanwhile, make the sauce. Gently heat the butter, cream and Parmesan in a medium saucepan until the butter and Parmesan have melted.

10 Increase the heat and simmer for a minute or two until the sauce is slightly reduced, then add salt and pepper to taste.

11 Drain the ravioli and divide them equally among eight warmed large bowls. Drizzle the sauce on them and serve sprinkled with Parmesan and ground pepper.

VARIATION

This cheese sauce would also work well with a baked pasta dish such as macaroni. Sprinkle the top generously with grated parmesan before baking.

Butter and Herb Sauce with Chitarra Spaghetti

YOU CAN USE JUST one favorite herb or several for this recipe. The result is the simplest way to dress up pasta but also one of the tastiest.

Serves 4

INGREDIENTS

14 ounces fresh or dried spaghetti
    alla chitarra
freshly grated Parmesan cheese, to serve

For the butter and herb sauce
2 good handfuls mixed fresh herbs, plus
    extra herb leaves and flowers to garnish
½ cup butter
salt and ground black pepper

1 Cook the pasta in boiling, lightly salted water according to the package instructions, until almost *al dente*.

2 To make the sauce, chop the herbs coarsely or finely, as you prefer.

3 When the pasta is almost *al dente*, melt the butter in a large frying pan or saucepan. As soon as it sizzles, drain the pasta and add it to the pan, then sprinkle in the herbs with salt and pepper to taste.

4 Toss over medium heat until the pasta is coated in butter and herbs. Serve immediately in warmed bowls, sprinkled with extra herb leaves and flowers. Pass some extra grated Parmesan separately.

VARIATION

If you like the flavor of garlic with herbs, add 1–2 crushed garlic cloves when melting the butter.

Bolognese Sauce with Ravioli

PERHAPS ONE OF THE most famous
pasta sauces outside Italy, Bolognese
sauce is a rich ragù from the city of
Bologna in Emilia-Romagna, an area
famous for fine foods.

Serves 6

INGREDIENTS

8 ounces cottage cheese
2 tablespoons freshly grated Parmesan
   cheese, plus extra for serving
1 egg white, beaten, including extra
   for brushing
¼ teaspoon ground nutmeg
11 ounces fresh pasta dough
all-purpose flour, for dusting

For the Bolognese sauce

1 medium onion, finely chopped
1 garlic clove, crushed
⅔ cup beef stock
12 ounces ground extra-lean beef
½ cup red wine
2 tablespoons concentrated tomato paste
14-ounce can chopped plum tomatoes
½ teaspoon chopped fresh rosemary
¼ teaspoon ground allspice
salt and ground black pepper

1 To make the filling, mix the cottage
cheese, grated Parmesan cheese, egg
white, seasoning and nutmeg thoroughly.

2 Roll the pasta into thin sheets, then
place small amounts of filling along
the pasta in rows, leaving a gap of
2 inches between them. Moisten around
the filling with beaten egg white.

3 Place a second sheet of pasta
lightly over the top. Press between
each pocket to remove air, and seal.

4 Cut into rounds with a fluted
ravioli or pastry cutter. Transfer to a
floured dish towel and let rest for at
least 30 minutes before cooking.

5 To make the Bolognese sauce, cook
the onion and garlic in the stock
for 5 minutes or until all the stock has
reduced. Add the beef and cook
quickly to brown, breaking up the meat
with a fork.

VARIATION

Stir in a handful of chopped chicken
livers with the ground beef to add a
more meaty richness to the sauce.

6 Add the wine, tomato paste,
chopped tomatoes, rosemary and
allspice. Bring to a boil and simmer for
1 hour. Season to taste.

7 Cook the ravioli in a large pan
of boiling, salted water for
4–5 minutes. (Cook in batches to
keep them from sticking together.)
Drain thoroughly. Serve topped with
the Bolognese sauce. Pass grated
Parmesan cheese separately.

Cream and Walnut Sauce on Pansotti

THIS WALNUT AND CREAM pesto is a simplified version of the one traditionally served with pansotti in Liguria. It would go equally well with any pasta stuffed with ricotta or spinach, or for a less rich alternative serve it with plain pasta shells.

Serves 6–8

INGREDIENTS
1¼ pounds herb-flavored pasta dough
*   with eggs*
¼ cup butter
freshly grated Parmesan cheese, to serve

For the filling
generous 1 cup ricotta cheese
1⅓ cups freshly grated
*   Parmesan cheese*
1 large handful fresh basil leaves,
*   finely chopped*
1 large handful fresh flat-leaf parsley,
*   finely chopped*
a few sprigs of fresh marjoram or oregano,
*   leaves removed and finely chopped*
1 garlic clove, crushed
1 small egg
salt and ground black pepper

For the cream and walnut sauce
1 cup shelled walnuts
1 garlic clove
4 tablespoons extra virgin olive oil
½ cup heavy cream

1 To make the filling, put the ricotta cheese, Parmesan cheese, basil, parsley, marjoram or oregano, garlic and egg in a bowl. Season with salt and ground black pepper to taste, and beat well to mix.

2 To make the sauce, put the walnuts, garlic clove and oil in a food processor and process into a paste, adding up to ½ cup warm water, through the feeder tube, to thin the paste.

3 Spoon the mixture into a bowl and add the cream. Beat well to mix, then season to taste.

4 Using a pasta machine, roll out one-quarter of the pasta into a 36–40-inch strip. Cut the strip with a sharp knife into two 18–20-inch lengths (you can do this during rolling if the strip gets too long to manage).

5 Using a 2-inch square ravioli cutter, cut eight to ten squares from one of the pasta strips.

6 Using a teaspoon, put a mound of filling in the center of each square.

7 Brush a little water around the edge of each square, then fold the square diagonally in half over the filling to make a triangle. Press gently to seal.

8 Spread out the pansotti on clean floured dish towels, sprinkle lightly with flour and set aside to dry, while repeating the process with the remaining dough, to make a total of 64–80 pansotti.

9 Cook the pansotti in a large pan of boiling salted water for 4–5 minutes.

10 Meanwhile, put the walnut sauce in a large, warmed bowl and add a ladleful of the pasta cooking water to thin it down. Melt the butter in a small saucepan until sizzling.

11 Drain the pansotti and put them in the bowl of walnut sauce. Drizzle the butter on them, toss well, then sprinkle with grated Parmesan. Alternatively, toss the pansotti in the melted butter, spoon into warmed individual bowls and drizzle on the sauce. Serve the dish immediately, with extra Parmesan passed separately.

COOK'S TIP

Be careful not to overfill the pansotti, or they will burst open during cooking.

Spinach Sauce with Seafood Pasta Shells

CREAM CHEESE AND SPINACH complement all kinds of pasta. This sauce would be perfect with any filled fresh pasta.

Serves 4

INGREDIENTS

32 large dried pasta shells

For the filling

1 tablespoon butter or margarine

8 scallions, finely sliced

6 tomatoes

8 ounces cooked peeled shrimp

6-ounce can white crabmeat, drained and flaked

For the spinach sauce

1 cup cream cheese

6 tablespoons milk

pinch of freshly grated nutmeg

4 ounces frozen chopped spinach, thawed and drained

salt and ground black pepper

1 Preheat the oven to 300°F. Melt the butter or margarine in a saucepan and cook the scallions for 3–4 minutes, until soft.

2 Plunge the tomatoes into boiling water for 1 minute, then into cold water. Slip off the skins. Halve the tomatoes, remove the seeds and cores and roughly chop the flesh.

3 Cook the pasta shells in lightly salted boiling water for about 10 minutes or until al dente. Drain.

4 To make the sauce, put the cream cheese and milk into a saucepan and heat gently, stirring until blended. Season with salt, ground black pepper and a pinch of nutmeg.

5 Measure 2 tablespoons of cheese mixture into a bowl. Add the scallions, tomatoes, shrimp, and crabmeat. Mix well. Spoon the filling into the shells and place in a single layer in a shallow ovenproof dish. Cover with aluminum foil and cook for 10 minutes.

6 Stir the spinach into the remaining sauce. Bring to a boil and simmer gently for 1 minute, stirring constantly. Drizzle on the pasta and serve hot.

Smoked Haddock and Parsley Sauce for Pasta

THIS HEARTY SAUCE made with smoked haddock makes any hollow pasta shape into a healthy lunch or supper. Shell-shaped pasta is ideal to hold the sauce, but corkscrew and tube shapes work just as well.

Serves 4

INGREDIENTS
8 ounces pasta shells
¹/₂ ounce toasted sliced almonds, to serve

For the smoked haddock and
parsley sauce
1 pound smoked haddock fillet
1 small leek or onion, thickly sliced
1¼ cups milk
bouquet garni (bay leaf, thyme and
    parsley stems)
2 tablespoons butter or margarine
¼ cup all-purpose flour
2 tablespoons chopped fresh parsley
salt and ground black pepper

3 Put the butter or margarine, flour and reserved milk into a pan. Bring to a boil and whisk until smooth. Season and add the fish and leek or onion.

4 Cook the pasta in a large pan of boiling salted water until *al dente*. Drain thoroughly and stir into the sauce with the chopped parsley. Serve immediately, with toasted sliced almonds.

1 Remove all the skin and any bones from the haddock and discard. Put into a pan with the leek or onion, milk and bouquet garni. Bring to a boil, cover and simmer gently for 8–10 minutes or until the fish flakes easily.

2 Strain, reserving the milk for making the sauce, and discard the bouquet garni.

Shrimp and Vodka Sauce with Pasta

THE COMBINATION OF SHRIMP, vodka and pasta may seem unusual, but has become a modern classic in Italy. Here it is served with two-colored pasta, but the sauce goes equally well with short shapes such as penne, rigatoni and farfalle.

Serves 4

INGREDIENTS
12 ounces fresh or dried paglia e fieno

For the shrimp and vodka sauce
2 tablespoons olive oil
1/4 large onion, finely chopped
1 garlic clove, crushed
1–2 tablespoons sun-dried tomato paste
scant 1 cup heavy cream
12 large raw shrimp, peeled and chopped
2 tablespoons vodka
salt and ground black pepper

1 Heat the oil in a medium saucepan, add the onion and garlic and cook gently, stirring frequently, for about 5 minutes or until softened.

2 Add the tomato paste and stir for 1–2 minutes, then add the cream and bring to a boil, stirring. Season with salt and pepper to taste and let the sauce bubble until it starts to thicken slightly. Remove from heat.

3 Cook the pasta according to the instructions on the package, until al dente. When it is almost ready, add the shrimp and vodka to the sauce; toss over medium heat for 2–3 minutes or until the shrimp turn pink.

4 Drain the pasta and turn it into a warmed bowl. Pour on the sauce and toss well. Divide among warmed bowls and serve immediately.

COOK'S TIP

This sauce is best served as soon as it is ready, otherwise the shrimp will overcook and become tough. Make sure that the pasta has only a minute or two of cooking time left before adding the shrimp to the sauce.

Smoked Salmon and Cream Sauce with Penne

THIS MODERN WAY OF serving pasta is popular all over Italy. The three essential ingredients combine beautifully, and the dish is very quick and easy to make.

Serves 4

INGREDIENTS
12 ounces penne

For the smoked salmon and cream sauce
4 ounces thinly sliced smoked salmon
2–3 fresh thyme sprigs
2 tablespoons butter
2/3 cup heavy cream
salt and ground black pepper

1 Cook the pasta in boiling salted water until it is al dente.

2 Meanwhile, using kitchen scissors, cut the smoked salmon into thin strips, about 1/4-inch wide. Strip the leaves from the thyme sprigs.

3 Melt the butter in a large saucepan. Stir in the cream with a quarter of the salmon and thyme leaves, then season with pepper. Heat gently for 3–4 minutes, stirring constantly. Do not let boil. Taste for seasoning.

4 Drain the pasta and toss it in the cream and salmon sauce. Divide among four warmed bowls and top with the remaining salmon and thyme leaves. Serve immediately.

VARIATION

Although penne is traditional with this sauce, it also goes very well with fresh ravioli stuffed with spinach and ricotta.

Spicy Sausage Sauce with Tortiglioni

SERVE THIS HEADY PASTA DISH with a robust Sicilian red wine.

Serves 4

INGREDIENTS

11 ounces dried tortiglioni
salt and ground black pepper

For the spicy sausage sauce

2 tablespoons olive oil
1 onion, finely chopped
1 celery stalk, finely chopped
2 large garlic cloves, crushed
1 fresh red chile, deseeded and chopped
1 pound ripe plum tomatoes, peeled and
    finely chopped
2 tablespoons tomato paste
⅔ cup red wine
1 teaspoon sugar
6 ounces spicy salami, rind removed
2 tablespoons chopped fresh parsley, to garnish
freshly grated Parmesan cheese, to serve

1 Heat the oil in a flameproof casserole or large saucepan, then add the onion, celery, garlic and chile. Cook gently, stirring frequently, for about 10 minutes, until softened.

2 Add the tomatoes, tomato paste, wine, sugar and salt and pepper to taste and bring to a boil, stirring. Lower the heat, cover and simmer gently, stirring occasionally, for about 20 minutes. Add a few spoonfuls of water if the sauce becomes too thick.

3 Meanwhile, cook the pasta in a large saucepan of rapidly boiling, salted water according to the instructions on the package, until al dente.

4 Chop the salami into bite-size chunks and add to the sauce. Heat through, then taste for seasoning.

5 Drain the pasta, put it in a large bowl, then pour on the sauce and toss to mix. Sprinkle on the parsley and serve with grated Parmesan.

COOK'S TIP

Buy the salami for this dish in one piece so that you can chop it into large chunks.

Wild Mushroom Sauce with Fusilli

A VERY RICH DISH with an earthy flavor and lots of garlic, this makes an ideal main course for vegetarians, especially if it is followed by a crisp green salad.

Serves 4

INGREDIENTS

5 ounces wild mushrooms preserved in olive oil
2 tablespoons butter
5 ounces fresh wild mushrooms, sliced if large
1 teaspoon finely chopped fresh thyme
1 teaspoon finely chopped fresh marjoram or oregano, plus extra herbs to serve
4 garlic cloves, crushed
12 ounces fresh or dried fusilli
scant 1 cup heavy cream
salt and ground black pepper

1 Drain about 1 tablespoon of the oil from the mushrooms into a medium saucepan. Slice or chop the preserved mushrooms into bite-size pieces, if they are large.

2 Add the butter to the oil in the pan and heat over low heat until sizzling. Add the preserved and the fresh mushrooms, the chopped herbs and the garlic. Season to taste.

SAFETY TIP

Unless you're an expert, or know of one who will identify them for you, it's safer not to pick mushrooms in the wild, but buy them instead from a reliable source.

3 Simmer over medium heat, stirring frequently, for about 10 minutes or until the fresh mushrooms are soft and tender.

4 Meanwhile, cook the pasta in boiling salted water according to the package instructions, until *al dente*.

5 As soon as the mushrooms are cooked, increase the heat to high and toss the mixture with a wooden spoon to boil off any excess liquid. Pour in the cream and bring to a boil. Season if needed.

6 Drain the pasta and turn it into a warmed bowl. Pour on the sauce and toss well. Serve immediately, sprinkled with chopped fresh herbs.

Sauces for Meat Dishes

The simplest, most basic sauce for meat is traditional gravy. Based on the juices from the cooked meat, this is one of the most widely used, everyday sauces. It is on this, together with a basic brown sauce, that many meat sauces are based, from classic French Espagnole sauce to rich Cumberland sauce flavored with port. But not only brown sauces are used with meat—you'll also find white, creamy sauces and a delicate butter in this section.

Many red meat dishes provide an opportunity for quite robust sauces, using warm spices, garlic or pungent herbs, simmered with red wine or tomato mixtures for added richness. The contrasting flavors of tangy fruits or sweet-and-sour mixtures are particularly successful with rich meats, such as beef, lamb, pork, venison or duck, including the popular combinations of duck with orange and venison with cranberries.

Although usually classed as a white meat, pork is also a natural partner for the tangy sweetness of apples or oranges, and pairs well with sweet-and-sour type sauces. More delicately flavored white meats or poultry, such as veal, chicken and turkey, go well with cream sauces or sauces based on white wine.

Avocado Sauce with Lemon Chicken

THIS GREAT SAUCE IS based on the classic Mexican dip, guacamole. Made without the addition of water, it could be used as a dip with raw vegetables, or even as a sandwich filling. Here it teams perfectly with chicken.

Serves 4

INGREDIENTS

juice of 2 lemons

3 tablespoons olive oil

2 garlic cloves, crushed

5 chicken breasts, about 7 ounces each

2 beefsteak tomatoes, cored and cut in half

salt and ground black pepper

For the avocado sauce

1 ripe avocado

¼ cup sour cream

3 tablespoons fresh lemon juice

½ teaspoon salt

¼ cup water

To serve

chopped cilantro, to garnish

1 Combine the lemon juice, oil, garlic, ½ teaspoon salt, and a little pepper in a bowl. Stir to mix.

2 Arrange the chicken breasts in one layer in a shallow glass or ceramic dish. Pour on the lemon mixture and turn to coat evenly. Cover and let stand for at least 1 hour at room temperature, or chill overnight.

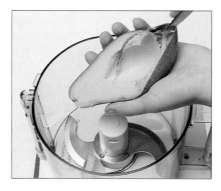

3 For the avocado sauce, cut the avocado in half, remove the pit and scrape the flesh into a food processor or blender.

4 Add the sour cream, lemon juice and salt, and process until smooth. Add the water and process just to blend. If necessary, add more water to thin the sauce. Transfer to a bowl, taste and adjust the seasoning, if necessary. Set aside.

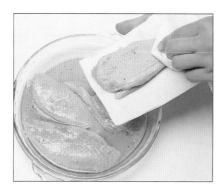

5 Preheat the broiler to hot. Heat a ridged griddle or heavy frying pan. Remove the chicken from the marinade and pat dry.

6 When the griddle or frying pan is hot, add the chicken breasts and cook, turning often, for about 10 minutes, until they are cooked through.

7 Meanwhile, arrange the tomato halves, cut-sides up, on a baking sheet and season lightly with salt and pepper. Broil for about 5 minutes, until hot and bubbling.

8 To serve, place a chicken breast, tomato half, and a spoonful of avocado sauce on each plate. Sprinkle with cilantro and serve.

VARIATION

To grill the chicken, prepare the grill, and, when the coals are glowing red and covered with gray ash, spread them in a single layer. Set an oiled grill rack about 5 inches above the coals and cook the chicken breasts for 15–20 minutes, until lightly charred and cooked through. Allow extra olive oil for basting.

Walnut and Pomegranate Sauce with Duck Breasts

THIS IS AN EXTREMELY EXOTIC sweet-and-sour sauce which originally comes from Iran.

Serves 4

INGREDIENTS

4 duck breasts, about 8 ounces each

For the walnut and pomegranate sauce
2 tablespoons olive oil
2 onions, very thinly sliced
½ teaspoon ground turmeric
2⅓ cups walnuts, roughly chopped
4 cups duck or chicken stock
6 pomegranates
2 tablespoons sugar
4 tablespoons lemon juice
salt and ground black pepper

1 To make the sauce, heat half the oil in a frying pan. Add the onions and turmeric, and cook gently until soft.

2 Transfer to a saucepan, add the walnuts and stock, then season with salt and pepper. Stir, then bring to a boil and simmer the mixture, uncovered, for 20 minutes.

3 Cut the pomegranates in half and scoop out the seeds. Reserve the seeds of one pomegranate. Transfer the remaining seeds to a blender and process to break them up. Strain through a sieve, to extract the juice, and stir in the sugar and lemon juice.

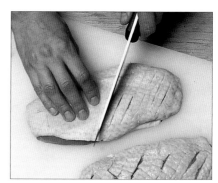

4 Score the skin of the duck breasts in a diamond pattern with a sharp knife. Heat the remaining oil in a frying pan or griddle and place the duck breasts in it, skin-side down.

5 Cook gently for 10 minutes, pouring off the fat, until the skin is dark golden and crisp. Turn the duck breasts over and cook for another 3–4 minutes. Transfer to a plate and let rest. Deglaze the frying pan with the pomegranate juice, then add the walnut and stock mixture and simmer for 15 minutes, until thickened.

6 Slice the duck and serve drizzled with a little sauce, and garnished with the reserved pomegranate seeds. Serve the remaining sauce separately.

Red Currant Sauce with Lamb Burgers

THE SWEET-AND-SOUR red currant sauce is a perfect complement to lamb and would go equally well with grilled or roast lamb steaks.

Serves 4

INGREDIENTS

1¼ pounds ground lean lamb
1 small onion, finely chopped
2 tablespoons finely chopped fresh mint
2 tablespoons finely chopped fresh parsley
4 ounces mozzarella cheese
2 tablespoons oil, for basting
salt and ground black pepper

For the red currant sauce

1 cup fresh or frozen red currants
2 teaspoons honey
1 teaspoon balsamic vinegar
2 tablespoons finely chopped mint

1 In a large bowl, mix the ground lamb, chopped onion, mint and parsley until evenly combined. Season well with plenty of salt and ground black pepper.

2 Roughly divide the meat mixture into eight equal pieces and use your hands to press each of the pieces into flat rounds.

3 Cut the mozzarella into four chunks. Place a chunk of cheese on half the lamb rounds. Top each with another round of meat mixture.

4 Press each of the two rounds of meat together firmly, making four flattish burger shapes. Use your fingers to blend the edges and seal in the cheese completely.

5 To make the sauce, place all the ingredients in a bowl and mash them together with a fork. Season well with salt and ground black pepper.

6 Brush the lamb burgers with olive oil and cook over a medium-hot grill for about 15 minutes, or broil for 10 minutes turning once, until golden brown. Serve with the sauce.

VARIATION

To make a quick version of the sauce, melt a jar of ready-made red currant sauce with balsamic vinegar and mint.

Pes

THE INTEN
and garlic
lamb, and
Parmesan
crust duri

Serves 6

INGREI

5–6-pound

For the pe

1¾ cups fr
4 garlic clo
3 tablespoo
⅔ cup olive
⅔ cup fresh
1 teaspoon

1 To mak
garlic an
processo
chopped.
slowly ad
Scrape th
the Parm

2 Set t
Make
a knife, a

Noisettes of Pork with Creamy Calvados and Apple Sauce

THIS DISH IS IDEAL AS part of a formal menu to impress guests. Buttered gnocchi or griddled polenta and red cabbage are suitable accompaniments.

Serves 4

INGREDIENTS

2 tablespoons plain flour

4 noisettes of pork, about 6 ounces each, firmly tied

1 ounce butter

4 baby leeks, finely sliced

1 teaspoon mustard seeds, coarsely crushed

2 tablespoons Calvados

¼ pint/⅔ cup dry white wine

2 Golden Delicious apples, peeled, cored and sliced

¼ pint/⅔ cup double cream

2 tablespoons chopped fresh parsley

salt and ground black pepper

1 Place the flour in a bowl and add plenty of seasoning. Turn the noisettes in the flour mixture to coat them lightly.

2 Melt the butter in a heavy-based frying pan and cook the noisettes until golden on both sides. Remove from the pan and set aside.

3 Add the leeks to the fat remaining in the pan and cook for 5 minutes. Stir in the mustard seeds and pour in the Calvados, then carefully ignite it to burn off the alcohol.

4 When the flames have died down pour in the wine and replace the pork. Cook gently for 10 minutes, turning the pork frequently.

5 Add the apples and cream and simmer for 5 minutes, or until the apples are tender. Taste for seasoning, then stir in the chopped parsley and serve at once.

Chili-nectarine Relish with Pork Chops

PORK AND FRUIT ARE a classic combination, and this spicy nectarine relish is the perfect partner for pork chops.

Serves 4

INGREDIENTS

1 cup fresh orange juice
3 tablespoons olive oil
2 garlic cloves, minced
1 teaspoon ground cumin
1 tablespoon coarsely ground black pepper
8 pork loin chops, about ¾-inch thick,
   well trimmed
salt

For the chili-nectarine relish

1 small fresh green chile pepper
2 tablespoons honey
juice of ½ lemon
1 cup chicken stock
2 nectarines, pitted and chopped
1 garlic clove, crushed
½ onion, finely chopped
1 teaspoon grated fresh ginger root
¼ teaspoon salt
1 tablespoon chopped cilantro

1 Roast the chile over a gas flame, holding it with tongs, until charred on all sides. (Alternatively, char the skin under the broiler.) Cool for 5 minutes.

2 Wearing rubber gloves, remove the charred skin of the chile. Discard seeds if a milder flavor is desired. Finely chop the chile and place in a pan.

3 Add the honey, lemon juice, chicken stock, nectarines, garlic, onion, ginger and salt. Bring to a boil, then simmer, stirring occasionally, for about 30 minutes. Stir in the cilantro and set aside.

4 In a small bowl, combine the orange juice, oil, garlic, cumin and pepper. Stir to mix.

5 Arrange the pork chops, in one layer, in a shallow dish. Pour on the orange juice mixture and turn to coat. Cover and let stand for at least 1 hour, or chill overnight.

6 Remove the pork from the marinade and pat dry with paper towels. Season lightly with salt.

7 Heat a frying pan or ridged griddle. Add the meat and cook for about 5 minutes or until browned. Turn and cook on the other side for about 10 more minutes. (Work in batches if necessary.) Serve immediately, with the relish.

COOK'S TIP

The relish can be made in advance, then covered and stored in the refrigerator overnight for the flavors to mature.

Sage and Orange Sauce with Pork Fillet

SAGE IS OFTEN PARTNERED with pork—there seems to be a natural affinity —and the addition of orange to the sauce balances the flavor.

Serves 4

INGREDIENTS
2 pork fillets, about 12 ounces each
2 teaspoons unsalted butter
salt and ground black pepper
orange wedges and sage leaves, to garnish

For the sage and orange sauce
¹/₂ cup dry sherry
³/₄ cup chicken stock
2 garlic cloves, very finely chopped
grated zest and juice of 1 unwaxed orange
3 or 4 sage leaves, finely chopped
2 teaspoons cornstarch

1 Season the pork fillets lightly with salt and pepper.

2 Melt the butter in a heavy, flame-proof casserole over medium-high heat, then add the meat and cook for 5–6 minutes, turning to brown all sides evenly.

3 Add the sherry, boil for about 1 minute, then add the stock, garlic, orange zest and chopped sage. Bring to a boil and reduce the heat to low, then cover and simmer for 20 minutes, turning once.

4 Transfer the pork to a warmed platter and cover to keep warm.

5 Bring the sauce to a boil. Blend the cornstarch and orange juice and stir into the sauce, then boil gently over medium heat for a few minutes, stirring frequently, until the sauce is slightly thickened.

6 Slice the pork diagonally and pour the meat juices into the sauce.

7 Spoon a little sauce onto the pork and garnish with orange wedges and sage leaves. Serve the remaining sauce separately.

COOK'S TIP

• The meat is cooked if the juices run clear when the meat is pierced, or when a meat thermometer inserted into the thickest part of the meat registers 150°F.
• If fresh sage is not available, try using rosemary as a substitute, as this also goes very well with pork.

Smoked Cheese Sauce with Veal Cutlets

SHEEP'S MILK CHEESE melted with cream makes a simple sauce for serving with pan-fried veal cutlets. The cutlets are used as purchased, not beaten thin.

Serves 4

INGREDIENTS

2 tablespoons butter

1 tablespoon extra virgin olive oil

8 small veal cutlets

2 garlic cloves, crushed

3$^{1}/_{2}$ cups button mushrooms or closed cup mushrooms, sliced

1$^{1}/_{4}$ cups frozen peas, thawed

4 tablespoons brandy

1 cup whipping cream

5 ounces smoked sheep's milk cheese, diced

salt and ground black pepper

sprigs of flat-leaf parsley, to garnish

1 Melt half the butter with the oil in a large, heavy frying pan. Season the cutlets with plenty of pepper and brown them in batches on each side over high heat. Reduce the heat and cook for about 5 minutes on each side until just done. The cutlets should feel firm to the touch, with a very light springiness.

2 Lift the cutlets onto a serving dish and keep hot.

3 Add the remaining butter to the pan. When it melts, stir-fry the garlic and mushrooms for about 3 minutes.

4 Add the peas, pour in the brandy and cook until all the pan juices have been absorbed. Season lightly. Using a slotted spoon, remove the mushrooms sand peas and place on top of the cutlets. Pour the cream into the pan.

5 Stir in the diced cheese. Heat gently until the cheese has melted. Season with pepper only and pour onto the cutlets and vegetables. Serve immediately, garnished with sprigs of flat-leaf parsley.

VARIATION

This dish works well with lean pork steaks. Ensure that pork is well cooked, with a slightly longer frying time.

Sweet-and-sour Sauce with Pork

2 Spread out the flour in a shallow bowl. Season well with salt and pepper and coat the meat.

3 Heat 1 tablespoon of the oil in a wide, heavy saucepan or frying pan and add as many slices of pork as the pan will hold. Fry over medium to high heat for 2–3 minutes on each side or until crispy and tender. Remove with a spatula and set aside. Repeat with the remaining pork, adding more oil as necessary.

THE COMBINATION OF SWEET-and-sour flavors is popular in Venetian cooking, especially with meat and liver. This recipe is given extra bite with the addition of crushed mixed peppercorns. Served with shelled fava beans tossed with bacon, it is delectable.

Serves 2

INGREDIENTS

1 whole pork fillet, about 12 ounces
1½ tablespoons all-purpose flour
2–3 tablespoons olive oil
salt and ground black pepper
fava beans tossed with bacon,
    to serve

For the sweet-and-sour sauce

1 cup dry white wine
2 tablespoons white wine vinegar
2 teaspoons sugar
1 tablespoon mixed peppercorns,
    coarsely ground

1 Cut the pork diagonally into thin slices. Place between two sheets of plastic wrap and pound lightly with a rolling pin to flatten them evenly.

4 Mix the wine, wine vinegar and sugar in a bowl. Pour into the pan and stir vigorously over high heat until reduced, scraping the pan to incorporate the sediment. Stir in the peppercorns and return the pork to the pan. Spoon the sauce onto the pork until it is evenly coated and heated through. Serve with the fava beans tossed with bacon.

COOK'S TIP

Grind the peppercorns in a pepper grinder, or crush them with a mortar and pestle.

Ham with Cumberland Sauce

CUMBERLAND SAUCE WAS INVENTED to honor the Duke of Cumberland, who commanded the troops at the last battle on English soil, against the Scots. It can be served hot or cold, with ham or venison.

Serves 8–10

INGREDIENTS

5 pounds smoked or unsmoked ham
1 onion
1 carrot
1 celery stalk
bouquet garni sachet
6 peppercorns

For the glaze
whole cloves
¹/₄ cup light brown sugar
2 tablespoons golden or light corn syrup
1 teaspoon English mustard powder

For the Cumberland sauce
juice and shredded zest of 1 orange
2 tablespoons lemon juice
¹/₂ cup port or red wine
4 tablespoons red currant jelly

2 Add the vegetables and seasonings, cover and simmer very gently for 2 hours. (The meat can also be cooked in the oven at 350°F. Allow 30 minutes per 1 pound.)

3 Let the meat cool in the liquid for 30 minutes. Then remove it from the liquid and strip off the skin neatly with the help of a knife (use rubber gloves if the ham is too hot to handle).

4 Score the fat in diamonds with a sharp knife and stick a clove in the center of each diamond. Preheat the oven to 350°F.

5 Put the sugar, golden syrup or light corn syrup and mustard powder in a small pan and heat gently to melt them. Place the ham in a roasting pan and spoon on the hot glaze. Bake it for about 20 minutes or until golden brown, then put it under a hot broiler to color.

6 Let the meat stand in a warm place for 15 minutes before carving (this makes carving much easier and tenderizes the meat).

7 For the Cumberland sauce, put the orange and lemon juice into a pan with the port or wine and red currant jelly, and heat gently to melt the jelly. Pour boiling water onto the orange zest, strain, and add the zest to the sauce. Cook gently for 2 minutes. Serve the sauce hot.

COOK'S TIP

Ham is often not as strongly salted as it once was, so it may not be necessary to soak overnight before cooking to remove the salty flavor.

1 Soak the ham overnight in a cool place in plenty of cold water to cover. Discard this water. Put the ham into a large pan and cover it again with more cold water. Bring the water to a boil slowly and skim any scum from the surface with a slotted spoon.

Cranberry Sauce with Venison

VENISON STEAKS ARE NOW readily available. Lean and low in fat, they make a healthy choice for a special occasion. Served with a sauce of fresh seasonal cranberries, port and ginger, they make a dish with a wonderful combination of flavors.

Serves 4

INGREDIENTS

2 tablespoons sunflower oil

4 venison steaks

2 shallots, finely chopped

salt and ground black pepper

fresh thyme sprigs, to garnish

creamy mashed potatoes and broccoli,
    to serve

For the cranberry sauce

1 orange

1 lemon

¾ cup fresh or frozen cranberries

1 teaspoon grated fresh ginger root

1 fresh thyme sprig

1 teaspoon Dijon mustard

4 tablespoons red currant jelly

⅔ cup port

1 For the sauce, pare the zest thinly from half the orange and half the lemon using a vegetable peeler, then cut into very fine strips.

2 Blanch the strips in a small pan of boiling water for about 5 minutes until tender. Strain the strips and refresh under cold water.

3 Squeeze the juice from the orange and lemon and then pour into a small pan. Add the fresh or frozen cranberries, ginger, thyme sprig, mustard, red currant jelly and port. Cook the sauce mixture over low heat until the jelly melts.

4 Bring the sauce to a boil, stirring occasionally, then cover the pan and reduce the heat. Cook gently, for about 15 minutes or until the cranberries are just tender.

5 Heat the oil in a heavy frying pan, add the venison steaks and cook over high heat for 2–3 minutes.

6 Turn over the steaks and add the shallots to the pan. Cook the steaks on the other side for 2–3 minutes, depending on whether you like rare or medium cooked meat.

7 Just before the end of cooking, pour in the sauce and add the strips of orange and lemon zest. Let the sauce bubble for a few seconds to thicken slightly, then remove the thyme sprig and adjust the seasoning to taste.

8 Transfer the venison steaks to warmed plates and spoon on the sauce. Garnish with thyme sprigs and serve accompanied by creamy mashed potatoes and broccoli.

COOK'S TIP

When frying venison, always remember the briefer the better; venison will turn to leather if subjected to fierce heat after it has reached the medium-rare stage. If you dislike any hint of pink, cook it to this stage, then let it rest in a low oven for a few minutes.

VARIATION

When fresh cranberries are unavailable, use red currants instead. Stir them into the sauce toward the end of cooking with the orange and lemon zests.

Gravy with Beef Pot Roast

A TRADITIONAL DISH that will feed a crowd at low cost. The rich gravy gathers all the flavor from the meat and vegetables, so nothing is wasted.

Serves 8

INGREDIENTS

4 pounds cut of beef suitable for pot
   roasting, such as brisket
3 garlic cloves, cut in half or in thirds
8-ounce piece salt pork or bacon
10 ounces onions, chopped
3 celery stalks, chopped
2 carrots, chopped
4 ounces turnip, diced
scant 2 cups beef or
   chicken stock
scant 2 cups dry red or white wine
1 bay leaf
1 teaspoon fresh thyme, or
   ½ teaspoon dried
4–6 small whole potatoes, or 3 large
   potatoes, quartered
3 ounces beurre manié
salt and ground black pepper
watercress, to garnish

1 Preheat the oven to 325°F. Make deep incisions in the beef on all sides with the tip of a sharp knife and insert the garlic pieces.

2 In a large, flameproof casserole, cook the salt pork or bacon over low heat until the fat runs and the pork or bacon begins to brown.

3 Remove the meat with a slotted spoon and discard. Increase the heat to medium-high and add the beef to the casserole. Brown it evenly on all sides. Remove and set aside on a plate or dish while you prepare the remaining vegetables.

4 Add the chopped onions, celery and carrots to the casserole and cook them for 8–10 minutes, stirring occasionally to avoid sticking, until all the vegetables are softened.

5 Stir in the diced turnips, add the beef or chicken stock, red or white wine, bay leaf and thyme, and mix well. Return the beef and any juices to the casserole, cover and cook in the preheated oven for 2 hours.

6 Add the whole or quartered potatoes to the casserole, pushing them down under the other vegetables. Season with salt and ground black pepper to taste. Cover the casserole once more and cook for another 45 minutes or until the potatoes are tender.

7 Transfer the meat to a warmed serving dish. Remove the potatoes and other vegetables from the casserole with a slotted spoon and arrange around the beef.

8 Discard the bay leaf and skim off excess fat from the cooking liquid.

9 Bring to a boil on the stove, then stir teaspoonfuls of the beurre manié into the liquid, whisking thoroughly to blend and adding just enough to thicken to taste. Strain into a gravy boat.

10 Serve the meat with some of the gravy poured on and the vegetables alongside. Garnish as desired with watercress. Offer the remaining gravy for pouring.

COOK'S TIP

Suitable cuts of beef for pot roasting include brisket, thin and thick rump, thick flank (top rump) and topside. Your butcher should be able to advise you.

VARIATION

For extra color, stir 6 ounces frozen peas into the casserole about 5 minutes before the potatoes are cooked.

Black Bean Sauce with Beef and Broccoli Stir-fry

THIS CHINESE BEEF DISH is a quick stir-fry with a richly flavored marinade that bubbles down into a luscious, dark sauce.

Serves 4

INGREDIENTS

8 ounces lean fillet or rump steak

1 tablespoon sunflower oil

8 ounces broccoli

4 ounces baby corn, diagonally halved

3–4 tablespoons water

2 leeks, diagonally sliced

8-ounce can water chestnuts, sliced

For the marinade

1 tablespoon fermented black beans

2 tablespoons dark soy sauce

2 tablespoons Chinese rice vinegar or cider vinegar

1 tablespoon sunflower oil

1 teaspoon sugar

2 garlic cloves, crushed

1-inch piece of fresh ginger root, peeled and finely chopped

1 To make the marinade, mash the fermented black beans in a non-metallic bowl. Add the remaining ingredients and stir well.

2 Cut the steak into thin slices across the grain, then add them to the marinade. Stir the steak well to coat it in the marinade. Cover the bowl and set aside for several hours.

3 Heat the oil in a large frying pan. Drain the steak (reserving the marinade). When the oil is hot, add the meat and stir-fry for 3–4 minutes. Transfer it to a plate and set aside.

4 Cut the broccoli into small florets. Reheat the oil in the pan, add the broccoli, corn and water. Cover and steam gently for 5 minutes.

5 Add the leeks and water chestnuts to the broccoli mixture and toss over the heat for 1–2 minutes. Return the meat to the pan, pour on the reserved marinade and toss briefly over high heat before serving.

COOK'S TIP

Fermented black beans are cooked, salted and fermented whole soy beans; they are available at Asian markets.

Roquefort and Walnut Butter with Rump Steak

MAKE A ROLL OF this savory cheese butter to keep in the refrigerator, ready to top plain steaks or pork chops.

Serves 4

INGREDIENTS

1 tablespoon finely snipped fresh chives
1 tablespoon olive oil or sunflower oil
4 lean rump steaks, about 4½ ounces each
½ cup dry white wine
2 tablespoons crème fraîche or heavy cream
salt and ground black pepper
fresh chives, to garnish

For the Roquefort and walnut butter
2 shallots, chopped
6 tablespoons butter, slightly softened
5 ounces Roquefort cheese
2 tablespoons finely chopped walnuts

1 Sauté the shallots in a third of the butter. Put in a bowl and add half the remaining butter, the cheese, walnuts, snipped chives and pepper to taste. Chill lightly, roll in aluminum foil into a sausage shape and chill again until firm.

2 Heat the remaining butter with the oil and cook the steaks to your liking. Season and remove from the pan.

3 Pour the wine into the pan and stir to incorporate any sediment. Bubble up the liquid for a minute or two, then stir in the crème fraîche or cream. Season with salt and pepper and pour onto the steaks.

4 Cut pats of the Roquefort butter from the roll and put one on top of each steak. Garnish with chives and serve. Green beans make an ideal accompaniment to this dish.

COOK'S TIP

The butter can also be stored in the freezer, but it is easier to cut it into rounds before freezing, so you can remove just as many as you need, without thawing the rest.

Sauces for Fish Dishes

You might expect all sauces for fish to be very delicate and light in flavor, but that's not always the case. Certainly in this chapter you'll find a classic white Parsley Sauce and a deliciously subtle Lemon and Chive Sauce: the perfect partners for white fish or fishcakes. But you'll also discover some more surprising combinations—a Tangy Orange and Caper Sauce to pep up plain white fish, and a Chili Barbecue Sauce to serve with salmon steaks.

There are some flavors that are natural partners for fish, such as lemon or dill, which can be used in classic white or white wine sauces, or in butters to serve with whole fish, fillets or steaks. Some of the classic pairings that have become enduring favorites cannot be ignored. The rich, oily flesh of mackerel balances perfectly with the tangy acidity of a Gooseberry Sauce, and the slightly sharp flavor of sorrel offsets the richness of salmon and transforms it into a sophisticated dinner-party dish.

As with any sauce, there are no hard-and-fast rules, but the general guideline is that white fish pairs best with subtle cream sauces and herb butters, whereas oily fish can take more robust flavors like spices or tangy fruits.

Orange and Caper Sauce with Skate

A WONDERFULLY SWEET-SOUR, creamy sauce to add zest to otherwise plain white fish.

Serves 4

INGREDIENTS

4 skate wings, about 7 ounces each
2 tablespoons butter
1½ cups fish stock

For the orange and caper sauce

2 tablespoons butter
1 onion, chopped
fish bones and trimmings
1 teaspoon black peppercorns
1¼ cups dry white wine
2 small oranges
1 tablespoon capers, drained
4 tablespoons crème fraîche
salt and ground white pepper

1 To make the sauce, melt the butter and add the onion. Sauté over medium heat until the onion is lightly browned.

2 To the sauce, add the fish bones and trimmings and peppercorns, then pour in the wine. Cover and simmer gently for 30 minutes.

3 Using a serrated knife, peel the oranges, ensuring that all the white pith is removed. Ease the segments away from the membrane.

4 Place the skate in a frying pan, add the butter and the fish stock and poach for 10–15 minutes, depending on thickness.

5 Strain the wine mixture into a clean saucepan. Add the capers and orange segments together with any juice, and heat through. Lower the heat and gently stir in the crème fraîche and seasoning. Serve the skate wings and the sauce, garnished with parsley.

VARIATION

For an unusual change, try using ruby grapefruit instead of the orange—this goes particularly well with oily fish such as trout or tuna.

Parsley Sauce with Haddock

ONE OF THE MOST classic sauces for fish is parsley sauce—a perfect partner for any white fish.

Serves 4

INGREDIENTS
4 haddock fillets, about 6 ounces each
2 tablespoons butter
⅔ cup milk
⅔ cup fish stock
1 bay leaf
salt and ground black pepper

For the parsley sauce
2 tablespoons butter
4 teaspoons all-purpose flour
4 tablespoons light cream
1 egg yolk
3 tablespoons chopped fresh parsley
grated zest and juice of ½ lemon

1 Place the fish in a frying pan, add the butter, milk, fish stock, bay leaf and seasoning, and heat to the simmering point.

2 Lower the heat, cover the pan and poach the fish for 10–15 minutes, depending on the thickness of the fillets, until the fish is tender and the flesh begins to flake. Transfer to a warm serving plate, cover and keep warm.

3 Make the sauce. Return the cooking liquid to the heat and bring to a boil, stirring. Simmer for about 4 minutes, then remove and discard the bay leaf.

4 Melt the butter in a saucepan, stir in the flour and cook, stirring continuously, for 1 minute.

5 Remove the pan from heat and gradually stir in the fish cooking liquid.

6 Return to the heat and bring to a boil, stirring. Simmer for about 4 minutes, stirring frequently.

7 Remove the pan from heat. In a bowl, blend the cream into the egg yolk, then stir this into the sauce with the parsley.

8 Reheat gently, stirring, for a few minutes; do not let boil.

9 Remove from heat and add the lemon juice and zest, and season to taste. Pour into a warmed sauceboat and serve with the fish.

Vermouth and Chèvre Sauce with Pan-fried Cod

2 Heat a nonstick frying pan, then add the oil, swirling it around to coat the bottom. Add the pieces of cod and cook, without turning or moving them, for 4 minutes or until nicely caramelized.

3 Turn each piece over and cook the other side for another 3 minutes, or until just firm. Remove them to a serving plate and keep hot.

4 To make the sauce, heat the oil and stir-fry the scallions for 1 minute. Add the vermouth and cook until reduced by half. Add the stock and cook again until reduced by half. Stir in the crème fraîche or cream and chèvre (goat's milk cheese) and simmer for 3 minutes.

A SMOOTH SAUCE OF vermouth and light, creamy chèvre teams deliciously with chunky, white cod.

Serves 4

INGREDIENTS

4 pieces of cod fillet, about 5 ounces
    each, skinned
salt and ground black pepper
fresh flat-leaf parsley, to garnish

For the vermouth and chèvre sauce

4 scallions, chopped
⅔ cup dry vermouth,
    preferably Noilly Prat
1 tablespoon olive oil
1¼ cups fish stock
3 tablespoons crème fraîche or
    heavy cream
2½ ounces chèvre (goat's milk cheese),
    rind removed, and chopped
2 tablespoons chopped fresh parsley
1 tablespoon chopped fresh chervil

1 Remove any stray bones from the cod fillets. Rinse the fish under cold running water and pat dry with paper towels. Place the pieces on a plate and season generously.

VARIATION

Instead of cod you could use salmon, haddock or plaice. The cooking time may change according to the thickness of the fish fillets.

5 Add salt and pepper to taste, stir in the herbs and spoon onto the fish. Garnish with parsley.

Dill and Mustard Sauce with Sole

THIS SAUCE WILL GIVE A TANGY, Scandinavian flavor that is perfect with grilled fish. Sole is used here, but the dill and mustard would combine with virtually any fish.

Serves 3–4

INGREDIENTS

3–4 lemon sole fillets
melted butter, for brushing
salt and ground black pepper
lemon slices and dill sprigs, to garnish

For the dill and mustard sauce
2 tablespoons butter
3 tablespoons all-purpose flour
1¼ cups hot fish stock
1 tablespoon white wine vinegar
3 tablespoons chopped fresh dill
1 tablespoon whole-grain mustard
2 teaspoons sugar
2 egg yolks

1 Preheat the broiler to medium-high. Brush the fish with melted butter, season on both sides and cut two or three slashes in the flesh. Grill for 4 minutes, then transfer to a warmed place and keep warm while you make the sauce.

2 Melt the butter over medium heat and stir in the flour. Cook for 1–2 minutes over low heat, stirring continuously to remove any lumps.

3 Remove from heat and gradually blend in the hot stock. Return to the heat, bring to a boil, stirring continuously, then simmer for 2–3 minutes.

VARIATION

A fennel and mustard sauce could also be made using chopped fennel leaves instead of the dill. Replace the whole-grain mustard with Dijon.

4 Remove the saucepan from heat and beat in the vinegar, dill, mustard and sugar.

5 Using a fork, beat the yolks in a small bowl and gradually add a small amount of hot sauce. Return to the pan, whisking vigorously. Continue whisking over very low heat for another minute. Serve immediately with the grilled sole, garnished with lemon slices and dill sprigs.

Gooseberry Sauce with Mackerel

GOOSEBERRIES AND MACKEREL ARE a classic combination; the tart sauce offsets the rich, oily fish.

Serves 4

INGREDIENTS

4 fresh mackerel, about 12 ounces
    each, cleaned
salt and ground black pepper

For the gooseberry sauce

1 tablespoon butter
8 ounces gooseberries, topped and tailed
1 egg, beaten
pinch of ground mace or ginger, or a few
    drops of orange flower water (optional)
fresh flat-leaf parsley, to garnish

1 Melt the butter in a saucepan, add the gooseberries, then cover and cook over low heat, shaking the pan until the gooseberries are just tender.

2 Meanwhile, preheat the broiler. Season the fish inside and out with salt and black pepper.

3 Cut two or three slashes in the skin on both sides of each mackerel, then broil for 15–20 minutes, or until cooked, turning once.

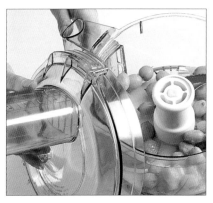

4 Purée the gooseberries with the egg in a food processor or blender, or mash the gooseberries thoroughly in a bowl with the egg. Press the gooseberry mixture through a sieve.

5 Return the gooseberry mixture to the pan and reheat gently, stirring, but do not let boil. Add the mace, ginger or orange flower water, if using, and season to taste. Serve the sauce hot with the mackerel, garnished with fresh parsley.

COOK'S TIPS

• For the best flavor, look for triple strength orange flower water, which can be obtained at good food stores.
• If fresh gooseberries are not in season, canned ones are an alternative. Make sure they do not contain added sugar, or the tart flavor will not be achieved.

Herb Sauce with Sardines

THE ONLY ESSENTIAL ACCOMPANIMENT to this luscious herb sauce is fresh, crusty bread to mop up the tasty juices. The sauce is also quite delicious served with plain, grilled chicken breasts. For the best flavor, grill the sardines.

Serves 4

INGREDIENTS

12–16 fresh sardines
oil, for brushing
juice of 1 lemon
crusty bread, to serve

For the herb sauce
1 tablespoon butter
4 scallions, chopped
1 garlic clove, finely chopped
grated zest of 1 lemon
2 tablespoons finely chopped fresh parsley
2 tablespoons finely snipped fresh chives
2 tablespoons finely chopped fresh basil
2 tablespoons green olive paste
2 teaspoons balsamic vinegar
salt and ground black pepper

3 Add the lemon zest and remaining sauce ingredients to the onions and garlic in the pan and keep warm on the edge of the stove or grill, stirring occasionally. Do not let the mixture boil.

4 Brush the sardines lightly with oil and sprinkle with lemon juice, salt and pepper. Grill for about 2 minutes on each side, over medium heat. Serve with the warm sauce and fresh crusty bread.

1 To clean the sardines, use a pair of small kitchen scissors to slit the fish along the belly and pull out the innards. Wipe the fish with paper towels and then arrange on a wire rack.

2 To make the sauce, melt the butter in a small pan and gently sauté the scallions and garlic for about 2 minutes, shaking the pan occasionally, until softened but not browned.

Tomato Coulis with Marinated Monkfish

A LIGHT BUT WELL-FLAVORED sauce, this should be made when Italian plum tomatoes are at their ripest. The lime and herb marinade is offset by the sweet tomatoes in the coulis. Serve this delicious dish with a glass of chilled white wine.

Serves 4

INGREDIENTS

2 tablespoons olive oil
finely grated zest and juice of 1 lime
2 tablespoons chopped fresh mixed herbs
1 teaspoon Dijon mustard
4 skinless, boneless monkfish fillets
salt and ground black pepper
fresh herb sprigs, to garnish

For the tomato coulis

4 plum tomatoes, peeled and chopped
1 garlic clove, chopped
1 tablespoon olive oil
1 tablespoon tomato paste
2 tablespoons chopped fresh oregano
1 teaspoon light brown sugar

1 Place the oil, lime zest and juice, herbs, mustard, and salt and pepper in a small bowl and whisk together until thoroughly mixed.

2 Place the monkfish fillets in a shallow, non-metallic container and pour on the lime mixture. Turn the fish several times in the marinade to coat it. Cover and chill in the refrigerator for 1–2 hours.

3 Meanwhile, make the tomato coulis. Place all the coulis ingredients in a food processor or blender and process until smooth. Season to taste, then cover and chill until needed.

4 Preheat the oven to 350°F. Using a spatula, place each fish fillet on a sheet of waxed paper big enough to hold it in a parcel.

5 Spoon a little marinade on each piece of fish. Gather the paper loosely over the fish and fold over the edges to secure the parcel tightly. Place on a baking sheet.

6 Bake for 20–30 minutes or until the fish fillets are cooked, tender and just beginning to flake.

7 Carefully unwrap the parcels and serve the fish fillets immediately with a little of the chilled coulis served alongside, and garnished with a few fresh herb sprigs.

COOK'S TIP

The coulis can be served hot, if you prefer. Simply make as directed in the recipe and heat gently in a saucepan until almost boiling, just before serving.

Watercress Cream with Poached Salmon

THE DELICATE GREEN COLOR of this cream sauce looks wonderful against pink-fleshed fish such as salmon or salmon trout.

Serves 4

INGREDIENTS

4 salmon fillets, about 6 ounces each
2 tablespoons butter
⅔ cup hot fish stock
⅔ cup dry white wine
1 bay leaf
salt
pinch cayenne pepper

For the watercress cream
2 bunches watercress
2 tablespoons butter
2 shallots, chopped
¼ cup all-purpose flour
1 teaspoon anchovy paste
⅔ cup light cream
lemon juice

VARIATION

To make arugula cream, replace the watercress with 1 ounce arugula leaves.

1 Trim the watercress of any bruised leaves and coarse stems. Blanch in boiling water for 5 minutes. Drain and refresh under cold running water. In a sieve, press with a spoon to remove excess moisture. Chop finely.

2 Place the fish in a saucepan, add the butter, the fish stock, wine, bay leaf and seasoning, and heat over low-medium heat to the simmering point.

3 Lower the heat, cover the pan and poach the fish for 10–15 minutes, depending on thickness, until tender.

4 Transfer to a warmed plate, cover and keep warm. Discard the bay leaf and reserve the cooking liquid for the sauce.

5 To make the sauce, melt the butter and sauté the shallots until soft. Stir in the flour and cook for 1–2 minutes.

6 Remove from heat and gradually blend in the reserved fish cooking liquid. Return to the heat, bring to a boil, stirring continuously, and simmer gently for 2–3 minutes.

7 Strain the sauce into a clean saucepan, then add the watercress, anchovy paste and cream. Warm over low heat. Season with salt and cayenne pepper and sharpen with lemon juice to taste. Serve immediately with the poached salmon.

Lemon and Chive Sauce
with Herbed Fishcakes

THIS PIQUANT SAUCE MAKES a delicious accompaniment to fishcakes but would also team well with most grilled or baked fish dishes.

Serves 4

INGREDIENTS

12 ounces potatoes, peeled
5 tablespoons skim milk
12 ounces haddock or hoki fillets, skinned
1 tablespoon lemon juice
1 tablespoon creamed horseradish sauce
2 tablespoons chopped fresh parsley
all-purpose flour, for dusting
2 cups fresh whole-wheat
   bread crumbs
salt and ground black pepper
sprigs of fresh flat-leaf parsley, to garnish
vegetables in season, to serve

For the lemon and chive sauce
thinly pared zest and juice of ½ small lemon
½ cup dry white wine
2 thin slices fresh ginger root
2 teaspoons cornstarch
2 tablespoons snipped fresh chives

1 Place the potatoes in a large saucepan of boiling water and cook for 15–20 minutes. Drain and mash with the milk, and season to taste.

2 Purée the fish with the lemon juice and horseradish sauce in a food processor or blender. Mix with the potatoes and parsley.

3 With floured hands, shape the mixture into eight fishcakes and coat with the bread crumbs. Chill in the refrigerator for 30 minutes.

4 Cook the fishcakes under a preheated medium-hot broiler for about 5 minutes on each side, until browned.

5 To make the sauce, cut the lemon zest into julienne strips and put into a large saucepan together with the lemon juice, wine and ginger, and season to taste.

6 Simmer the sauce uncovered for 6 minutes.

7 Blend the cornstarch with 1 tablespoon of cold water. Add to the ingredients in the saucepan and simmer, stirring, until the sauce has thickened and is clear.

8 Stir in the chives immediately before serving. Serve the sauce hot with the fishcakes. Garnish the dish with sprigs of flat-leaf parsley and serve with a selection of vegetables.

Sorrel Sauce with Salmon Steaks

THE SHARP FLAVOR OF the sorrel sauce balances the richness of the fish. The young plant has the mildest flavor, so try to buy the herb in spring when it is at its best.

Serves 2

INGREDIENTS

2 salmon steaks, about 9 ounces each
1 teaspoon olive oil
salt and ground black pepper
fresh sage, to garnish

For the sorrel sauce
1 tablespoon butter
2 shallots, finely chopped
3 tablespoons crème fraîche
3¹/₂ ounces fresh sorrel leaves, washed
*   and patted dry*

1 Season the salmon steaks with salt and pepper. Brush a nonstick frying pan with the oil.

2 Make the sauce. In a small saucepan, melt the butter over medium heat. Add the shallots and sauté for 2–3 minutes, stirring frequently, until just softened.

3 Add the crème fraîche and the sorrel leaves to the shallots and cook until the sorrel is completely wilted, stirring constantly.

4 Meanwhile, place the frying pan over medium heat until hot. Add the salmon steaks and cook for about 5 minutes, turning once, until the flesh is opaque next to the bone. If you're not sure, pierce the flesh with the tip of a sharp knife; the fish should flake easily.

5 Arrange the salmon steaks on two warmed plates, garnish with sage and serve with the sorrel sauce.

COOK'S TIP

If preferred, cook the salmon steaks in the microwave for 4–5 minutes, in a tightly covered dish, or according to the manufacturer's guidelines.

VARIATION

If sorrel is not available, use finely chopped watercress instead.

Chili Barbecue Sauce with Salmon

THIS SPICY TOMATO AND mustard sauce is delicious served with grilled salmon fillets—cook them either on a grill or under a hot broiler.

Serves 4

INGREDIENTS

4 salmon fillets, about 6 ounces

For the chili barbecue sauce

2 teaspoons butter
1 small red onion, finely chopped
1 garlic clove, finely chopped
6 plum tomatoes, diced
3 tablespoons ketchup
2 tablespoons Dijon mustard
2 tablespoons dark brown sugar
1 tablespoon honey
1 teaspoon ground cayenne pepper
1 tablespoon ancho chili powder
1 tablespoon ground paprika
1 tablespoon Worcestershire sauce

1 To make the barbecue sauce, melt the butter in a large, heavy saucepan and gently cook the chopped onion and garlic until they are tender and translucent.

2 Stir in the tomatoes and simmer for 15 minutes, stirring occasionally (to break up the tomato pieces).

3 Add the remaining sauce ingredients and simmer for another 20 minutes.

4 Process the mixture until smooth, in a food processor fitted with a metal blade. Let cool.

5 Brush the salmon with the sauce and chill for at least 2 hours. Grill or broil 2–3 minutes on either side, brushing on the sauce when necessary. Serve drizzled with the remaining sauce.

Butter Sauce with Salmon Cakes

THIS LEMONY BUTTER SAUCE keeps the salmon fishcakes deliciously moist; they make a real treat for supper or a leisurely breakfast at the weekend.

Makes 6

INGREDIENTS

8-ounce tail piece of salmon, cooked
2 tablespoons chopped fresh parsley
2 scallions, trimmed and chopped
2⅔ cups firm mashed potatoes
1 egg, beaten
1 cup fresh white bread crumbs
butter and oil, for frying (optional)
salt and ground black pepper

For the butter sauce
6 tablespoons butter
grated zest and juice of ½ lemon

1 Remove all the skin and bones from the fish and mash or flake it well. Add the chopped parsley, onions and 1 teaspoon of the lemon zest (from the same ingredients) and season with salt and black pepper.

2 Gently work in the potato, and then shape into six rounds.

3 Chill the fishcakes for 20 minutes to let them firm up. Coat each fishcake well in egg and then the bread crumbs. Broil gently for 5 minutes on each side, or until golden, or fry in butter and oil over medium-hot heat.

4 To make the butter sauce, in a saucepan, melt the butter over low heat, then whisk in the remaining lemon zest and the lemon juice, together with 1–2 tablespoons cold water. Season with salt and ground black pepper to taste. Simmer the sauce for a few minutes, and then serve immediately with the fish cakes.

VARIATION

If desired, use a lime instead of the half lemon for a change of flavor. This butter sauce is a quick and easy accompaniment to virtually any fish.

COOK'S TIP

Tail pieces of salmon fillet are usually a good buy and do not contain bones, but any cut of salmon can be used for this dish, so look for any that are on sale.

Seafood with Warm Green Tartar Sauce

A COLORFUL SAUCE THAT'S good with all kinds of seafood, particularly fresh scallops, and looks stunning over black pasta.

Serves 4

INGREDIENTS

12 ounces black tagliatelle
12 large scallops
4 tablespoons white wine
⅔ cup fish stock
lime wedges and parsley sprigs, to garnish

For the warm green tartare sauce

½ cup crème fraîche
2 teaspoons whole-grain mustard
2 garlic cloves, crushed
2–3 tablespoons fresh lime juice
4 tablespoons chopped fresh parsley
2 tablespoons snipped chives
salt and ground black pepper

4 Put the white wine and fish stock into a saucepan. Heat to the simmering point. Add the scallops and cook very gently for 3–4 minutes (no longer, or they will become tough).

5 Remove the scallops from the saucepan. Boil the wine and stock to reduce by half and add the tartar sauce to the pan. Heat gently to warm the sauce.

6 Replace the scallops and cook for 1 minute. Spoon onto the pasta and garnish with lime wedges and parsley.

COOK'S TIPS

• If you are removing the scallops from the shells yourself, remember to wash them first in plenty of cold water.
• If the scallops are frozen, defrost them before cooking, as they will probably have been glazed with water and will need to be drained well.

VARIATIONS

• This sauce could be made equally well with fresh mussels.
• Instead of serving over pasta, this sauce would go particularly well with fish dishes, such as monkfish, which has a flavor reminiscent of lobster.

1 To make the tartar sauce, blend the crème fraîche, mustard, garlic, lime juice, parsley, chives and seasoning together in a food processor or blender.

2 Cook the pasta in a large pan of boiling, salted water according to the instructions on the package until al dente. Drain thoroughly.

3 Meanwhile, slice the scallops in half, horizontally. Keep any corals whole.

Romesco Sauce with Broiled Jumbo Shrimp

THIS SAUCE, FROM THE Catalan region of Spain, is served with fish and shellfish. Its main ingredients are sweet bell pepper, tomatoes, garlic and toasted almonds.

Serves 4

INGREDIENTS

24 raw jumbo shrimp
2–3 tablespoons olive oil
fresh flat-leaf parsley, to garnish
lemon wedges, to serve

For the romesco sauce
2 well-flavored tomatoes
4 tablespoons olive oil
1 onion, chopped
4 garlic cloves, chopped
1 canned pimiento, chopped
½ teaspoon dried chile flakes or powder
5 tablespoons fish stock
2 tablespoons sherry or white wine
10 blanched almonds
1 tablespoon red wine vinegar
salt

1 To make the sauce, immerse the tomatoes in boiling water for about 30 seconds, remove from the pan with a slotted spoon, then refresh them under cold water. Peel off the skins and roughly chop the flesh.

2 Heat 2 tablespoons of the oil in a pan, add the onion and 3 of the garlic cloves, and cook until soft.

3 Add the pimiento, tomatoes, chile, fish stock and sherry or wine, then cover and simmer for 30 minutes. Let cool slightly.

4 Meanwhile, toast the almonds under the broiler until golden.

5 Transfer the almonds to a blender or food processor and grind coarsely.

6 Add the remaining 2 tablespoons of oil, the vinegar and the last garlic clove and process the mixture until it is evenly combined.

7 Carefully add the tomato and pimiento sauce (in batches if necessary) and process until smooth. Season with salt to taste and return to the rinsed pan to keep warm.

8 Remove the heads from the shrimp, leaving them otherwise unshelled. With a sharp knife, slit each one down the back and remove the dark vein. Rinse and pat dry on paper towels. Preheat the broiler.

9 Toss the shrimp in olive oil, then spread out in a broiler pan. Broil for 2–3 minutes on each side, until pink. Arrange the shrimp on a serving platter and garnish with parsley. Serve immediately with the lemon wedges, and the sauce in a small bowl.

VARIATION

In Catalonia, romesco sauce is also served with local spicy sausages, grilled fish and poultry dishes. Spoonfuls can also be added to enrich a fish or chicken stew, much like a rouille is used in French cooking.

Five-spice and Black Bean Sauce with Stir-fried Squid

THIS SPICY ASIAN SAUCE is the ideal accompaniment for stir-fried squid and is very easy to make. It is important to have all the ingredients ready before you start to cook. The squid must be cooked very quickly, or it will toughen.

Serves 6

INGREDIENTS

1 pound small squid cleaned

3 tablespoons oil

For the five-spice and black bean sauce

1-inch piece fresh ginger root, grated

1 garlic clove, crushed

8 scallions, cut diagonally into
    1-inch lengths

1 red bell pepper, seeded and cut into strips

1 fresh green chile, seeded and thinly sliced

6 chestnut mushrooms, sliced

1 teaspoon five-spice powder

2 tablespoons black bean sauce

2 tablespoons soy sauce

1 teaspoon sugar

1 tablespoon rice wine or dry sherry

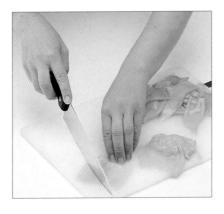

1 Rinse the squid and pull off the outer skin. Dry on paper towels. Slit the squid open and score the outside into diamonds with a sharp knife. Cut the squid into strips.

2 Heat a wok and add the oil. When it is hot, stir-fry the squid quickly. Remove the squid strips from the wok with a slotted spoon and set aside.

3 For the sauce, add the ginger, garlic, scallions, red pepper, chile and mushrooms to the oil remaining in the wok and stir-fry for 2 minutes.

4 Return the squid to the wok and stir in the five-spice powder. Stir in the black bean sauce, soy sauce, sugar and rice wine or sherry. Bring to a boil and cook, stirring, for 1 minute. Serve immediately.

Tartar Sauce with Crab Cakes

WHEN SERVING ANY FRIED fish, tartar sauce is the traditional accompaniment, but it is also delicious with vegetables. Maryland is renowned for its seafood, and these little crab cakes hail from there.

Serves 4

INGREDIENTS

1½ pounds fresh white crabmeat

1 egg, beaten

2 tablespoons mayonnaise

1 tablespoon Worcestershire sauce

1 tablespoon sherry

2 tablespoons finely chopped fresh parsley

1 tablespoon finely chopped fresh chives

3 tablespoons olive oil

salt and ground black pepper

For the tartar sauce

1 egg yolk

1 tablespoon white wine vinegar

2 tablespoons Dijon-style mustard

1 cup vegetable or
    peanut oil

2 tablespoons fresh lemon juice

3 tablespoons finely chopped scallions

2 tablespoons chopped drained capers

3 tablespoons finely chopped dill pickles

3 tablespoons finely chopped fresh parsley

1 Pick over the crabmeat, removing any shell or cartilage. Keep the pieces of crab as large as possible.

2 In a bowl, combine the beaten egg with the mayonnaise, Worcestershire sauce, sherry and herbs. Season to taste. Gently fold in the crabmeat.

3 Divide the mixture into eight portions and gently form each into an oval cake.

4 Place on a baking sheet between layers of waxed paper and chill for at least 1 hour.

5 To make the sauce, in a bowl, beat the egg yolk with a wire whisk. Add the vinegar, mustard, and seasoning, and whisk for about 10 seconds. Whisk in the oil in a slow, steady stream.

6 Add the lemon juice, scallions, capers, dill pickles and parsley and mix well. Check the seasoning. Cover and chill.

7 Preheat the broiler. Brush the crab cakes with the olive oil. Place on an oiled baking sheet, in one layer. Broil 6 inches from heat until golden brown, about 5 minutes on each side. Alternatively, fry the crab cakes over medium heat for a few minutes on each side. Serve the crab cakes hot with the tartar sauce.

COOK'S TIPS

For easier handling and to make the crabmeat go further, add 1 cup fresh bread crumbs and 1 more egg to the crab mixture. Divide the mixture into 12 cakes to serve 6. Use dill instead of chives, if you prefer.

Sauces for Vegetarian Dishes

Vegetable dishes have until recently been considered the poor-relation of meat-based cooking, but it is not only vegetarians that are becoming more interested in making vegetable dishes more appetizing and interesting. All those interested in healthy eating are including more vegetable-based meals in their diet.

Vegetables are some of the most versatile ingredients—they can provide hearty, cold-weather meals, such as Baked Squash and Parsley Sauce, the family favorite of Cheddar Cheese Sauce with Cauliflower as well as light summer dishes consisting of steamed and fresh vegetables, such as Warm Vegetable Salad served with Peanut Sauce.

The sauces in this chapter, however, are not intended to be served exclusively with vegetable meals. They provide flavor and texture that can be teamed with freshly cooked pasta, such as the Green Vegetable Sauce and polenta, and the Wild Mushroom Sauce. Others provide a piquant flavor to a plainer dish, like Citrus Sauce or Mustard Sauce, which add spice to liven up zucchini or potatoes but would be equally at home with fish or meat dishes. Any of these sauces will enhance and complement a variety of dishes —whether the flavors are similar or contrasting—if you choose carefully.

Mustard Sauce with Potato Skewers

THIS THICK, GARLIC-RICH dipping sauce is versatile enough to serve with any vegetable kebab or even with crudités.

Serves 4

INGREDIENTS

2¼ pounds small new potatoes

7 ounces shallots, halved

2 tablespoons olive oil

1 tablespoon sea salt

For the mustard sauce

4 garlic cloves, crushed

2 egg yolks

2 tablespoons lemon juice

1¼ cups extra virgin olive oil

2 teaspoons whole-grain mustard

salt and ground black pepper

1 To make the mustard sauce, place the garlic, egg yolks and lemon juice in a food processor or blender and process briefly until smooth.

2 With the motor running, add the oil until the mixture forms a thick cream. Add the mustard, and season.

3 Parboil the potatoes in salted boiling water for about 5 minutes. Drain well and then thread them onto metal skewers with the shallots.

4 Brush the vegetable skewers lightly with olive oil and sprinkle with sea salt.

5 Cook the vegetables for 10–12 minutes over a hot grill or under the preheated broiler, turning often, until tender. Serve immediately with the mustard dipping sauce.

Chili Sauce with Spicy Potato Wedges

FOR A HEALTHY SNACK with superb flavor, try these dry-roasted potato wedges. The crisp spice crust makes them irresistible, especially when served with this chili sauce.

Serves 2

INGREDIENTS

2 baking potatoes, about 8 ounces
   each, unpeeled
2 tablespoons olive oil
2 garlic cloves, crushed
1 teaspoon ground allspice
1 teaspoon ground coriander
1 tablespoon paprika
sea salt and ground black pepper

For the chili sauce

1 tablespoon olive oil
1 small onion, finely chopped
1 garlic clove, crushed
7-ounce can chopped tomatoes
1 fresh red chile, seeded and finely chopped
1 tablespoon balsamic vinegar
1 tablespoon chopped cilantro, plus extra to
   garnish

1 Preheat the oven to 400°F. Cut the potatoes in half, then into eight wedges.

2 Place the wedges in a saucepan of cold water. Bring to a boil, then lower the heat and simmer gently for 10 minutes or until the potatoes have softened slightly. Drain well and pat dry on paper towels.

3 Mix the oil, garlic, allspice, coriander and paprika in a roasting pan. Add salt and pepper to taste. Add the potatoes to the pans and shake to coat them thoroughly. Roast for 20 minutes, turning the potato wedges occasionally, until they are browned, crisp and fully cooked.

4 Meanwhile, make the chili sauce. Heat the oil in a saucepan, add the onion and garlic and cook for 5–10 minutes, until soft. Add the chopped tomatoes, with their juice. Stir in the chile and vinegar.

5 Cook gently for 10 minutes or until the mixture has reduced and thickened, then check the seasoning. Stir in the cilantro and serve hot, with the potato wedges. Garnish with salt and cilantro.

COOK'S TIPS

• To save time, the potatoes can be parboiled and tossed with the spices in advance.
• Make sure that the potato wedges are perfectly dry and completely covered in the mixture before roasting.

Peanut Sauce with Warm Vegetable Salad

THIS SPICY SAUCE IS based on the classic Indonesian sauce served with saté, but is equally delicious served with this main-course salad, which mixes steamed and raw vegetables. It would also go well with vegetable kebabs.

Serves 2–4

INGREDIENTS

8 new potatoes

8 ounces broccoli, cut into small florets

1⅓ cups fine green beans

2 carrots, cut into thin ribbons with a
   vegetable peeler

1 red bell pepper, seeded and cut into strips

2 ounces sprouted beans

sprigs of watercress, to garnish

For the peanut sauce

1 tablespoon sunflower oil

1 birdseye chile, seeded and sliced

1 garlic clove, crushed

1 teaspoon ground coriander

1 teaspoon ground cumin

4 tablespoons crunchy peanut butter

5 tablespoons water

1 tablespoon dark soy sauce

½-inch piece fresh ginger root,
   finely grated

1 teaspoon dark brown sugar

1 tablespoon lime juice

4 tablespoons coconut milk

1 First, make the peanut sauce. Heat the oil in a saucepan, add the chile and garlic, and cook for 1 minute, until softened. Add the spices and cook for 1 minute.

2 Stir in the peanut butter and water, then cook for 2 minutes, or until combined, stirring constantly.

3 Add the soy sauce, ginger, sugar, lime juice and coconut milk, then cook over low heat until smooth and heated through, stirring frequently. Transfer to a bowl.

4 Bring a saucepan of lightly salted water to a boil, add the potatoes and cook for 10–15 minutes until tender. Drain, then halve or thickly slice the potatoes, depending on their size.

5 Meanwhile, steam the broccoli and green beans for 4–5 minutes, until tender but still crisp. Add the carrots 2 minutes before the end of the cooking time.

6 Arrange the cooked vegetables on a serving platter with the red pepper and sprouted beans. Garnish with watercress and serve with the peanut sauce.

COOK'S TIP

Adjust the dipping consistency by adding slightly less water than recommended; you can always stir in a little more at the last minute. Serve the sauce either warm or cold.

Baked Squash with Parsley Sauce

THIS IS A REALLY glorious way with a simple and modest vegetable. Try to find a small, firm and unblemished squash for this recipe, as the flavor will be sweet, fresh and delicate. Young squash do not need peeling; more mature ones do.

Serves 4

INGREDIENTS

1 small young summer squash, about 2 pounds
2 tablespoons olive oil
1 tablespoon butter
1 onion, chopped
1 tablespoon all-purpose flour
1¼ cups milk and light cream, mixed
2 tablespoons chopped fresh parsley
salt and ground black pepper

1 Preheat the oven to 350°F and cut the squash into pieces measuring about 2 x 1 inches.

2 Heat the oil and butter in a flame-proof casserole and sauté the onion over low heat until very soft.

3 Add the squash and sauté for 1–2 minutes and then stir in the flour. Cook for a few minutes.

6 Cover and cook for 30–35 minutes. If desired, uncover for the final 5 minutes of cooking to brown the top. Alternatively, serve the squash in its rich, pale sauce.

VARIATION

Chopped fresh basil or a mixture of basil and chervil also tastes good in this dish.

5 Add the parsley and seasoning, and stir well.

4 Stir the milk and cream into the vegetable mixture.

Roasted Bell Pepper Sauce with Malfatti

A SMOKY BELL PEPPER AND tomato sauce adds the finishing touch to spinach and ricotta dumplings. The Italians call these malfatti (badly made) because of their uneven shape.

Serves 4

INGREDIENTS

1¼ pounds young leaf spinach
1 onion, finely chopped
1 garlic clove, crushed
1 tablespoon extra virgin olive oil
1½ cups ricotta cheese
3 eggs, beaten
scant 1 cup dried bread crumbs
½ cup all-purpose flour
⅔ cup freshly grated
    Parmesan cheese
freshly grated nutmeg
2 tablespoons butter, melted

For the roasted bell pepper sauce
2 red bell peppers, seeded and quartered
2 tablespoons extra virgin olive oil
1 onion, chopped
14-ounce can chopped tomatoes
⅔ cup water
salt and ground black pepper

1 Make the sauce. Preheat the broiler and broil the pepper quarters skin-side up until they blister and blacken. Cool slightly, then peel off the skins and chop the flesh.

2 Heat the oil in a saucepan and lightly sauté the onion and peppers for 5 minutes.

3 Add the tomatoes and water, with salt and pepper to taste. Bring to a boil, lower the heat and simmer gently for 15 minutes.

4 Purée the mixture in a food processor or blender, in batches if necessary, then return to the clean pan and set aside.

5 Trim any thick stems from the spinach, wash it well if necessary, then blanch in a pan of boiling water for about 1 minute. Drain, refresh under cold water and drain again. Squeeze dry, then chop finely.

6 Put the finely chopped onion, garlic, olive oil, ricotta, eggs and bread crumbs in a bowl. Add the spinach and mix well. Stir in the flour and 1 teaspoon salt with half the Parmesan, then season to taste with pepper and nutmeg.

7 Roll the mixture into 16 small logs and chill lightly.

8 Bring a large saucepan of water to a boil. Carefully drop in the malfatti in batches and cook them for 5 minutes. Remove with a spatula and toss with the melted butter.

9 To serve, reheat the sauce and divide it among four plates. Arrange four malfatti on each and sprinkle on the remaining Parmesan. Serve immediately.

Quick Tomato Sauce with Baked Polenta with Cheese

THIS QUICK TOMATO SAUCE can be prepared from staple ingredients. The rich flavor of the sauce enhances baked polenta.

Serves 4

INGREDIENTS

1 teaspoon salt

2¼ cups quick-cook polenta

1 teaspoon paprika

½ teaspoon ground nutmeg

¾ cup grated Gruyère cheese

For the quick tomato sauce

2 tablespoons olive oil

1 large onion, finely chopped

2 garlic cloves, crushed

2 14-ounce cans chopped tomatoes

1 tablespoon tomato paste

1 teaspoon sugar

salt and ground black pepper

1 Preheat the oven to 400°F. Line an 11 x 7-inch baking pan with plastic wrap. Bring 4 cups of water to a boil with the measured salt.

2 Pour in the quick-cook polenta in a steady stream and cook, stirring continuously, for 5 minutes. Beat in the paprika and nutmeg, then pour into the prepared pan and smooth the surface. Let cool.

3 To make the quick tomato sauce, heat the oil in a pan and cook the onion and garlic until soft. Add the chopped tomatoes, tomato paste and sugar. Season, and simmer for 20 minutes.

4 Turn out the polenta onto a board, and cut into 2-inch squares. Place half the squares in a greased ovenproof dish. Spoon on half the tomato sauce, and sprinkle with half the cheese. Repeat the layers. Bake for 25 minutes.

Fresh Tomato and Ginger Sauce with Tofu and Potato Rösti

IN THIS RECIPE, the tofu is marinated in a mixture of tamari, honey and oil, flavored with garlic and ginger. This marinade is then added to the fresh tomatoes to make a thick, creamy tomato sauce with a delicious tang, and the method ensures that the tofu is infused with the same flavors.

Serves 4

INGREDIENTS

15 ounces tofu, cut into 1/2-inch cubes
4 large potatoes, about 2 pounds total
    weight, peeled
sunflower oil, for frying
salt and ground black pepper
2 teaspoons sesame seeds, toasted

For the fresh tomato and ginger sauce

2 tablespoons tamari or dark soy sauce
1 tablespoon honey
2 garlic cloves, crushed
1 1/2-inch piece fresh ginger root, grated
1 teaspoon toasted sesame oil
1 tablespoon olive oil
8 tomatoes, halved, seeded and chopped

1 For the sauce, mix the tamari or dark soy sauce, honey, garlic, ginger and toasted sesame oil in a shallow dish.

2 Add the tofu, then spoon the liquid onto the tofu and let marinate in the refrigerator for at least 1 hour. Turn the tofu occasionally in the marinade to let the flavors infuse.

3 To make the rösti, parboil the potatoes for 10–15 minutes, until almost tender. Let cool, then grate coarsely. Season well with salt and freshly ground black pepper. Preheat the oven to 400°F.

4 Using a slotted spoon, remove the tofu from the marinade and reserve the marinade on one side. Spread out the tofu on a baking tray and bake for 20 minutes, turning occasionally, until golden and crisp on all sides.

5 Take a quarter of the potato mixture in your hands at a time and form into rough cakes.

6 Heat a frying pan with just enough oil to cover the bottom. Place the cakes in the frying pan and flatten the mixture, using your hands or a spatula to form rounds about 1/2 inch thick.

7 Cook for about 6 minutes or until golden and crisp underneath. Carefully turn over the rösti and cook for another 6 minutes, until golden brown in color.

8 Meanwhile, complete the sauce. Heat the oil in a saucepan, add the reserved marinade and then the tomatoes and cook for 2 minutes, stirring continuously.

9 Reduce the heat and simmer, covered, for 10 minutes, stirring occasionally, until the tomatoes break down. Press the mixture through a sieve to make a thick, smooth sauce.

10 To serve, place a rösti on each of four warm serving plates. Sprinkle the tofu on top, spoon on the tomato sauce and sprinkle with sesame seeds.

COOK'S TIPS

• Tamari is a thick, mellow-flavored Japanese soy sauce, which is sold at Japanese and some larger health-food stores.
• Tofu can be rather bland, so let it marinate for 2–3 hours, if possible, to ensure that it is full of flavor.

Cheddar Cheese Sauce with Cauliflower

SELECT A FARMHOUSE Cheddar to give this popular dish a full flavor, and season with plenty of ground black pepper.

Serves 4

INGREDIENTS

2½ pounds cauliflower florets
   (about 1 large head)
3 bay leaves

For the Cheddar cheese sauce
3 tablespoons butter
3 tablespoons all-purpose flour
scant 2 cups milk
3 cups grated aged
   Cheddar cheese
salt and ground black pepper

1 Preheat the oven to 350°F. Grease a 12-inch round ovenproof dish.

2 Bring a large pan of lightly salted water to a boil. Add the cauliflower florets and cook for 7–8 minutes or until just tender but still firm. Drain well.

3 To make the sauce, melt the butter in a heavy saucepan. Whisk in the flour until blended with the butter. Cook until smooth and bubbling, stirring continuously.

4 Gradually add the milk. Bring to a boil and continue cooking, stirring constantly, until the sauce is thickened and smooth.

5 Remove from heat and stir in the cheese. Season the sauce to taste with salt and pepper.

6 Place the bay leaves on the bottom of the prepared dish. Arrange the cauliflower florets on top in an even layer. Pour the cheese sauce evenly onto the cauliflower.

7 Bake for 20–25 minutes or until golden brown and bubbling. Serve immediately.

VARIATION

You might like to try this with broccoli instead of cauliflower, or with a mixture of the two for a colorful change.

Wild Mushroom Sauce with Polenta and Gorgonzola

THE FLAVOR OF WILD mushrooms combines well with mascarpone in this sauce to heighten the taste of the polenta. It also makes a delicious topping for baked potatoes.

Serves 4–6

INGREDIENTS

3¾ cups milk
3¾ cups water
1 teaspoon salt
2¾ cups polenta
¼ cup butter
4 ounces Gorgonzola cheese
fresh thyme sprigs, to garnish

For the wild mushroom sauce

scant 1 cup dried
   porcini mushrooms
⅔ cup hot water
2 tablespoons butter
1½ cups button
   mushrooms, chopped
4 tablespoons dry white wine
generous pinch of dried thyme
4 tablespoons mascarpone cheese
salt and ground black pepper

1 Pour the milk and water into a large, heavy saucepan. Add the salt and bring to a boil. Using a long-handled spoon, stir the liquid briskly with one hand while drizzling in the polenta with the other. When the mixture is thick and smooth, lower the heat to a gentle simmer and cook for about 20 minutes, stirring occasionally.

2 Remove from heat and stir in the butter and Gorgonzola. Spoon the polenta mixture into a shallow dish and level the surface.

3 Let the polenta set until solid, then cut into wedges.

4 Meanwhile, make the sauce. Soak the porcini in the hot water for 15 minutes. Drain, reserving the liquid. Finely chop the porcini and strain the soaking liquid through a sieve lined with paper towels. Discard the paper towels.

5 Melt half the butter in a small saucepan. Sauté the chopped fresh mushrooms for about 5 minutes.

6 Add the wine, porcini and strained soaking liquid, with the dried thyme. Season to taste. Cook for 2 more minutes. Stir in the mascarpone and simmer for a few minutes, until reduced by a third. Set aside to cool.

7 Heat a ridged grill pan or broil, and cook the polenta until crisp. Brush with melted butter and serve hot with the sauce. Garnish with thyme.

COOK'S TIP

If fresh porcini mushrooms are available, use instead of dried and do not soak. You would need about 6 ounces fresh porcini for this recipe. They are also sold under the name cèpes.

Pineapple and Passion Fruit Salsa

PILE THIS SWEET, FRUITY salsa into brandy snap baskets or meringue nests for a luxurious dessert.

Serves 6

INGREDIENTS

1 small fresh pineapple
2 passion fruit
²/₃ cup plain yogurt
2 tablespoons light brown sugar

3 Halve the passion fruit and use a spoon to scoop out the seeds and pulp into a bowl.

4 Stir in the chopped pineapple and the yogurt. Cover and chill until needed.

5 Stir in the brown sugar just before serving the salsa.

VARIATION

Lightly whipped heavy cream can be used instead of yogurt.

1 Cut off the top and bottom of the pineapple so that it will stand firmly on a cutting board. Using a large, sharp knife, slice off the peel.

2 Use a small, sharp knife to carefully cut out the eyes. Slice the peeled pineapple and use a small cookie cutter to cut out the tough core. Finely chop the flesh.

Plantain Salsa

HERE IS A SUMMERY SALSA that is perfect for lazy outdoor eating. Serve with grilled meat or fish or with potato or vegetable chips or taco chips for dipping.

Serves 4

INGREDIENTS

pat of butter
4 ripe plantains
handful of cilantro, plus extra
  to garnish
2 tablespoons olive oil
1 teaspoon cayenne pepper
salt and ground black pepper

COOK'S TIP

Be sure to choose ripe plantains with blackened skins for this recipe, as they will be at their sweetest and most tender.

1 Preheat the oven to 400°F.

2 Grease four pieces of aluminum foil, each measuring roughly 6 x 8 inches, with a pat of butter.

3 Peel the plantains and place one on each piece of buttered foil. Carefully fold the pieces of foil over the plantain, sealing them tightly to form four parcels.

4 Bake the plantain for 25 minutes or until tender. Alternatively, the plantain may be cooked in the embers of a grill.

5 Let the parcels cool slightly, then remove the plantains, discarding any liquid, and place in a food processor or blender.

6 Process the plantains with the cilantro until fairly smooth. Stir in the olive oil, cayenne pepper, and salt and pepper to taste.

7 Serve immediately, as the salsa will discolor and over-thicken if left to cool for too long. Garnish with torn cilantro leaves.

Corn Salsa

SERVE THIS SUCCULENT SALSA with smoked meats or a juicy ham steak.

Serves 4

INGREDIENTS

2 ears of corn
2 tablespoons melted butter
4 tomatoes
6 scallions, finely chopped
1 garlic clove, finely chopped
2 tablespoons fresh lemon juice
2 tablespoons olive oil
red Tabasco sauce, to taste
salt and ground black pepper
scallion slices, to garnish

1 Remove the husks and silky threads covering the corn. Brush the corn with the melted butter and gently grill or broil for 20–30 minutes, turning occasionally, until tender and tinged brown.

2 To remove the kernels, stand the corn upright on a cutting board and use a large, heavy knife to slice down the length of the corn.

3 Skewer the tomatoes in turn on a metal fork and hold in a gas flame for 1–2 minutes, turning, until the skin splits and wrinkles. Slip off the skin and dice the tomato flesh.

4 Mix the scallions and garlic with the corn and tomato in a small bowl.

5 Mix the lemon juice, olive oil and Tabasco. Season to taste.

6 Pour this onto the salsa and stir well. Cover the salsa and let infuse at room temperature for 1–2 hours before serving, garnished with slices of scallion.

COOK'S TIP

Make this salsa in late summer when fresh corn is readily available and at the peak of flavor.

Berry Salsa

THIS UNUSUAL, RICHLY COLORED fruit salsa is the perfect choice for a summer *al fresco* meal, to serve with grilled or broiled fish or poultry.

Serves 4

INGREDIENTS

1 fresh jalapeño pepper

½ red onion, minced

2 scallions, chopped

1 tomato, finely diced

1 small yellow bell pepper, seeded and minced

3 tablespoons chopped cilantro

¼ teaspoon salt

1 tablespoon raspberry vinegar

1 tablespoon fresh orange juice

1 teaspoon honey

1 tablespoon olive oil

1½ cups strawberries, hulled

1½ cups blueberries or blackberries

generous 1 cup raspberries

1 Wearing rubber gloves, finely chop the jalapeño pepper (discard the seeds and membrane if a less hot flavor is desired). Place the pepper in a medium-size bowl.

2 Add the red onion, scallions, tomato, pepper and cilantro, and stir to blend.

3 In a small bowl, whisk together the salt, vinegar, orange juice, honey and olive oil. Pour onto the jalapeño mixture and stir well.

4 Coarsely chop the strawberries. Add to the jalapeño mixture with the other berries and stir to blend.

5 Let stand at room temperature for 3 hours, then serve.

COOK'S TIP

Defrosted frozen berries can be used in the salsa, but the texture will be softer.

Mixed Melon Salsa

A COMBINATION OF TWO **very**
different melons gives this salsa an
exciting flavor and texture. Try it
with thinly sliced prosciutto or
smoked salmon.

Serves 10

INGREDIENTS

1 small orange-fleshed melon,
  such as Charentais
1 large wedge watermelon
2 oranges

VARIATION

Other melons can be used for this salsa.
Try cantaloupe, Galia or Ogen.

1 Quarter the orange-fleshed melon
and remove the seeds. Use a large,
sharp knife to cut off the skin. Dice the
melon flesh.

2 Pick out the seeds from the
watermelon, then remove the skin.
Dice the flesh into small chunks.

3 Use a zester to pare long strips of
zest from both oranges. Halve the
oranges and squeeze out all their juice.

4 Mix both types of the melon and
the orange zest and juice in a bowl.
Chill for about 30 minutes and serve.

Roasted Bell Pepper and Ginger Salsa

2 Over medium heat, gently dry-fry the coriander and cumin for 30 seconds to 1 minute, shaking the pan to make sure they don't scorch.

3 Crush the spices in a mortar and pestle. Add the ginger and garlic and continue to work into a pulp. Work in the lime or lemon juice.

GRILLING TO REMOVE the skins will take away any bitterness from the peppers and soften the flesh. Serve the salsa with grilled vegetable kebabs.

Serves 6

INGREDIENTS

1 large red bell pepper
1 large yellow bell pepper
1 large orange bell pepper
½ teaspoon coriander seeds
1 teaspoon cumin seeds
1-inch piece ginger root, chopped
1 small garlic clove, chopped
2 tablespoons lime or lemon juice
1 small red onion, finely chopped
2 tablespoons cilantro, chopped
1 teaspoon fresh thyme, chopped
salt and ground black pepper

1 Preheat the broiler to hot. Quarter the peppers and remove the stem, seeds and membranes. Broil the quarters, skin-side up, until charred and blistered. Rub off the skins and slice very finely.

COOK'S TIP

If you don't have a mortar and pestle, crush the garlic and grate the ginger root. The spices can be ground in a pepper mill or crushed with a rolling pin.

4 Mix the peppers, spice mixture, onion and herbs. Season to taste with salt and ground black pepper and spoon into a serving bowl. Chill for 1–2 hours before serving as an accompaniment to grilled meats or kebabs.

Orange and Chive Salsa

FRESH CHIVES AND SWEET oranges provide a refreshing combination of flavors. This salsa can be used to cool down spicy grilled meat or poultry.

Serves 4

INGREDIENTS

2 large oranges
1 beefsteak tomato
bunch of chives
1 garlic clove, thinly sliced
2 tablespoons olive oil
sea salt

1 Slice the bottom off one orange so that it will stand firmly on a cutting board. Using a large, sharp knife, remove the peel by slicing from the top to the bottom of the orange.

2 Hold the orange over a bowl. Slice toward the middle of the fruit, to one side of a segment, and then twist the knife to ease the segment from the membrane and out of the orange. Repeat to remove all segments. Squeeze any juice from the membrane.

3 Prepare the second orange in the same way. Roughly chop the orange segments and place them in the bowl with the collected juice.

4 Halve the tomato and use a teaspoon to scoop the seeds into the bowl. Finely dice the flesh and add it to the oranges, juice and seeds in the bowl.

5 Hold the bunch of chives together and use a pair of scissors to snip them into the bowl. Stir in the garlic.

6 Pour the olive oil over, season with sea salt to taste and stir well to mix. Serve within 2 hours.

Mango and Red Onion Salsa

4 Carefully turn the skin inside out so the flesh stands out. Slice the dice away from the skin. Place in a bowl.

5 Finely chop the red onion and place it in the bowl with the mango. Halve the passion fruit, scoop out the seeds and pulp, and add to the mango mixture in the bowl.

A VERY SIMPLE TROPICAL salsa, which is livened up by the addition of passion fruit pulp. This salsa goes well with salmon and poultry.

Serves 4

INGREDIENTS

1 large ripe mango
1 red onion
2 passion fruit
6 large fresh basil leaves
juice of 1 lime, to taste
sea salt

1 Holding the mango upright on a cutting board, use a large knife to slice the flesh from each side of the large flat pit in two portions.

2 Using a smaller knife, trim off any flesh still clinging to the top and bottom of the pit.

3 Score the flesh of the mango halves deeply, taking care to avoid cutting through the skin: make parallel incisions about ½ inch apart; turn and cut lines in the opposite direction.

6 Tear the basil leaves coarsely and stir them into the mixture with lime juice and a little sea salt to taste. Mix well and serve the salsa immediately.

VARIATION

Freshly cooked corn kernels are a delicious addition to this salsa.

Aromatic Peach and Cucumber Salsa

ANGOSTURA BITTERS ADD AN unusual and very pleasing flavor to this salsa. The distinctive, sweet taste of the mint complements chicken and other meat dishes.

Serves 4

INGREDIENTS

2 peaches

1 mini cucumber

½ teaspoon angostura bitters

1 tablespoon olive oil

2 teaspoons fresh lemon juice

2 tablespoons chopped fresh mint

salt and ground black pepper

1 Using a small, sharp knife, carefully score a line right around the center of each peach, taking care to cut just through the skin.

2 Bring a large pan of water to a boil. Add the peaches and blanch them for 1 minute. Drain and briefly refresh in cold water. Peel off and discard the skin. Halve the peaches and remove their pits. Finely dice the flesh and place in a bowl.

3 Trim the ends off the cucumber, then finely dice the flesh and stir it into the peaches. Stir the angostura bitters, olive oil and lemon juice together and then stir this dressing into the peach mixture.

VARIATION

Use diced mango instead of the peaches for an alternative.

4 Stir in the mint with salt and pepper to taste. Chill and serve within 1 hour.

COOK'S TIP

The texture of the peach and the crispness of the cucumber will fade fairly rapidly, so try to prepare this salsa as close to serving time as possible.

Dips

Far from being just for parties, dips are for any occasion, any time of day and any season. They are an opportunity for informal eating, an appetite teaser and a very healthy way to snack. They're also a good choice for packed lunches and picnics, as they travel well and can be served in so many ways.

Hot or cold, dips are a very versatile food; they are invariably quick to make and uncomplicated, so they're easily rustled up at a moment's notice. For a satisfying treat, try a warm, creamy cheese Fonduta with crusty bread for dipping, or Hot Chili Bean Dip. Or, for a light, refreshing summer snack, serve Blue Cheese Dip or creamy Guacamole with fresh crudités. For parties, choose a selection of different dips for variety, so there's something for everyone's taste.

Serve your favorite dips with raw vegetable crudités, such as carrot, cucumber or celery sticks, raw mushrooms or cauliflower florets. Cooked vegetables, such as asparagus, artichokes or deep-fried mushrooms are just incomplete without a creamy or tangy savory dip. Or, try dipping fingers of pita bread, breadsticks and taco chips, perfect for easy snacking.

Saffron Dip

2 Beat the fromage frais until smooth, then stir in the infused saffron liquid.

3 Use a pair of scissors to snip the chives into the dip. Tear the basil leaves into small pieces and stir them in.

SERVE THIS MILD DIP with fresh vegetable crudités—it is particularly good with florets of cauliflower.

Serves 4

INGREDIENTS

1 tablespoon boiling water
small pinch of saffron threads
scant 1 cup fromage frais
10 fresh chives
10 fresh basil leaves
salt and ground black pepper

VARIATION

Leave out the saffron and add a squeeze of lemon or lime juice instead. A pinch of turmeric gives a good color.

1 Pour the boiling water into a small container and add the saffron threads. Let infuse for 3 minutes.

4 Add salt and pepper to taste. Serve the dip immediately.

Basil and Lemon Mayonnaise

THIS FRESH MAYONNAISE is flavored with lemon and two types of basil. Serve as a dip with potato wedges or crudités, or as an accompaniment to salads and baked potatoes.

Serves 4

INGREDIENTS

2 large egg yolks
1 tablespoon lemon juice
⅔ cup olive oil
⅔ cup sunflower oil
handful of green basil leaves
handful of dark opal (purple) basil leaves
4 garlic cloves, crushed
salt and ground black pepper
green and dark opal basil leaves and
   sea salt, to garnish

COOK'S TIP

Dark opal basil has crinkled, deep-purple leaves and a richly scented flavor, with a hint of black currants.

1 Place the egg yolks and lemon juice in a food processor or blender and process them briefly together.

2 In a pitcher, stir the two oils together. With the machine running, pour in the oil very slowly, a drop at a time.

3 Once half the oil has been added, the remainder can be incorporated more quickly. Continue processing the mixture to form a thick and creamy mayonnaise.

4 Tear both types of basil into small pieces and stir into the mayonnaise with the crushed garlic and seasoning. Transfer to a serving dish, cover and chill until ready to serve, garnished with basil leaves and sea salt.

Blue Cheese Dip

2 Add the cream cheese and beat well to blend the two cheeses together.

3 Gradually beat in the yogurt, adding enough to give you the consistency you desire.

4 Season with lots of black pepper and a little salt. Chill the dip until you are ready to serve it.

THIS DIP CAN BE mixed up in next to no time and is delicious served with pears, or with fresh vegetable crudités. Add more yogurt to make a great dressing. This is a very thick dip to which you can add a little more Greek-style yogurt, or stir in a little milk, for a softer consistency.

Serves 4

INGREDIENTS

5 ounces blue cheese, such as Stilton
   or Danish blue
⅔ cup cream cheese
5 tablespoons plain yogurt
salt and ground black pepper

1 Crumble the blue cheese into a bowl. Using a wooden spoon, beat the cheese to soften it.

Mellow Garlic Dip

TWO WHOLE HEADS OF garlic may seem like a lot, but roasting transforms the flesh to a tender, sweet and mellow pulp. Serve with crunchy breadsticks and chips. For a low-fat version of this dip, use reduced-fat mayonnaise and low-fat yogurt.

Serves 4

INGREDIENTS

2 whole garlic heads
1 tablespoon olive oil
4 tablespoons mayonnaise
5 tablespoons yogurt
1 teaspoon whole-grain mustard
salt and ground black pepper

1 Preheat the oven to 400°F. Separate the garlic cloves and place them in a small roasting pan.

2 Pour the olive oil onto the garlic cloves and turn them with a spoon to coat them evenly. Roast them for 20–30 minutes or until tender and softened. Let cool for 5 minutes.

3 Trim off the root end of each roasted garlic clove. Peel the cloves and discard the skins. Place the roasted garlic on a cutting board and sprinkle with salt. Mash with a fork until puréed.

4 Place the garlic in a small bowl and stir in the mayonnaise, yogurt and whole-grain mustard.

5 Check and adjust the seasoning, then spoon the dip into a bowl. Cover and chill until ready to serve.

COOK'S TIP

If you are cooking on a grill, leave the garlic heads whole and cook until tender, turning occasionally. Peel and mash.

Butternut Squash and Parmesan Dip

THE RICH, NUTTY FLAVOR of butternut squash is enhanced by roasting. Serve this dip with melba toasts or cheese straws.

Serves 4

INGREDIENTS

1 butternut squash
1 tablespoon butter
4 garlic cloves, unpeeled
2 tablespoons freshly grated
   Parmesan cheese
3–5 tablespoons heavy cream
salt and ground black pepper

1 Preheat the oven to 400°F.

2 Halve the butternut squash, then scoop out and discard the seeds.

3 Use a small, sharp knife to deeply score the flesh in a criss-cross pattern: cut as close to the skin as possible, without cutting through it.

4 Arrange both halves in a small roasting pan and dot them with the butter. Sprinkle the butternut squash with salt and ground black pepper and roast over high heat near the top of the oven for 20 minutes.

5 Tuck the unpeeled garlic cloves around the squash in the roasting pan and continue baking for 20 minutes, until the butternut squash is tender and softened.

6 Scoop the flesh out of the squash shells and place it in a food processor or blender. Slip the garlic cloves out of their skins and add to the squash. Process until smooth.

7 With the motor running, add all but 1 tablespoon of the Parmesan cheese and then the cream. Check the seasoning and spoon the dip into a serving bowl; it is at its best served warm. Sprinkle the reserved cheese on top. If you don't have a food processor or blender, mash the squash in a bowl using a potato masher, then beat in the cheese and cream with a wooden spoon.

VARIATION

Try making this dip with pumpkin or other types of squash, such as acorn squash or New Zealand kabocha. Adjust the cooking time depending on size.

Thousand Island Dip

This variation on the **classic** dressing is far removed from the original version, but can be served in the same way—with grilled jumbo shrimp laced onto bamboo skewers for dipping or with a simple mixed seafood salad.

Serves 4

INGREDIENTS

4 sun-dried tomatoes in oil
4 tomatoes
²/₃ cup cream cheese
4 tablespoons mayonnaise
2 tablespoons tomato paste
2 tablespoons chopped fresh parsley
grated zest and juice of 1 lemon
red Tabasco sauce, to taste
1 teaspoon Worcestershire or soy sauce
salt and ground black pepper

1 Drain the sun-dried tomatoes on paper towels to remove excess oil, then finely chop them.

2 Skewer each tomato in turn on a metal fork and hold in a gas flame for 1–2 minutes or until the skin wrinkles and splits. Let cool, then slip off and discard the skins. Halve the tomatoes and scoop out the seeds with a teaspoon. Finely chop the tomato flesh and set aside.

3 In a bowl, beat the cream cheese, then gradually beat in the mayonnaise and tomato paste to make a smooth mixture.

4 Stir in the chopped parsley and sun-dried tomatoes, then add the chopped tomatoes and their seeds, and mix well.

5 Add the lemon zest and juice and Tabasco sauce to taste. Stir in the Worcestershire or soy sauce, and salt and pepper to taste.

6 Transfer the dip to a serving bowl, cover and chill until ready to serve.

VARIATION

Stir in cayenne pepper or a chopped fresh chili for a more fiery dip. Garnish with a small piece of lemon, if desired.

Dips

Guacamole

THIS IS QUITE A fiery version of the popular Mexican dish, although probably nowhere near as hot as the dish you would be served in Mexico, where it often seems that heat knows no bounds! Serve it as a snack with tortilla chips or breadsticks.

Serves 4

INGREDIENTS

2 ripe avocados

2 tomatoes, peeled, seeded and finely chopped

6 scallions, finely chopped

1–2 chiles, seeded and finely chopped

2 tablespoons fresh lime or lemon juice

1 tablespoon chopped cilantro

salt and ground black pepper

cilantro sprigs, to garnish

1 Cut the avocados in half and remove the pits and discard. Scoop the flesh into a large bowl and mash it roughly with a large fork.

COOK'S TIP

Unless you are going to serve the dip immediately, cover the surface closely with a piece of plastic wrap to prevent it from browning. If the surface should still start to brown, stir lightly before serving.

2 Add the tomatoes, scallions, chiles, lime or lemon juice and cilantro. Mix well and season with salt and ground black pepper to taste.

3 Serve as soon as possible, garnished with cilantro.

VARIATION

For extra flavor, stir in a crushed garlic clove, or season with garlic salt.

Spiced Carrot Dip

THIS IS A DELICIOUS dip with a sweet and spicy flavor. Serve wheat crackers or fiery tortilla chips as accompaniments for dipping.

Serves 4

INGREDIENTS

1 onion

3 carrots, plus extra to garnish

grated zest and juice of 2 oranges

1 tablespoon hot curry paste

handful of fresh basil leaves

⅔ cup plain yogurt

1–2 tablespoons fresh lemon juice, to taste

red Tabasco sauce, to taste

salt and ground black pepper

3 Stir in the yogurt. Tear the basil leaves into small pieces and add most of them to the carrot mixture.

4 Add the lemon juice, Tabasco and seasoning. Serve within a few hours at room temperature, garnished with grated carrot and basil.

VARIATION

Sour cream may be used instead of the yogurt to make a richer, creamier-textured dip.

1 Finely chop the onion. Peel and grate the carrots. Place the onion, carrots, orange zest and juice, and curry paste in a small pan. Bring to a boil, cover and simmer for 10 minutes.

2 Process the mixture in a blender until smooth. Let cool.

Creamy Eggplant Dip

SPREAD THIS VELVET-TEXTURED DIP thickly onto toasted rounds of bread, then top them with slivers of sun-dried tomato to make wonderful, Italian-style crostini.

Serves 4

INGREDIENTS

1 large eggplant
2 tablespoons olive oil
1 small onion, finely chopped
2 garlic cloves, finely chopped
4 tablespoons chopped fresh parsley
5 tablespoons crème fraîche
red Tabasco sauce, to taste
juice of 1 lemon, to taste
salt and ground black pepper

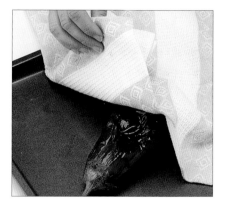

1 Preheat the broiler to medium. Place the whole eggplant on a nonstick baking sheet and broil it for 20–30 minutes under medium-high heat, turning occasionally, until the skin is blackened and wrinkled, and the eggplant feels soft when squeezed.

2 Cover the eggplant with a clean dish towel and let it cool for about 5 minutes.

3 Heat the oil in a frying pan and cook the onion and garlic for 5 minutes, until they are softened but not browned.

4 Peel the skin from the eggplant. Mash the flesh with a large fork or potato masher to make a pulpy purée.

5 Stir in the onion and garlic, parsley and crème fraîche. Add Tabasco, lemon juice, and salt and pepper to taste.

6 Transfer the dip to a serving bowl and serve warm or let cool and serve at room temperature.

COOK'S TIP

The eggplant can be roasted in the oven at 400°F for 20 minutes, or until tender, if preferred.

Hot Chili Bean Dip

MAKE THIS ONE AS hot as you like—
the sour cream helps to balance the
heat of the chiles. Serve it with
tortilla chips or vegetable crudités.

Serves 4

INGREDIENTS

1½ cups dried pinto beans, soaked
    overnight and drained
1 bay leaf
3 tablespoons sea salt
1 tablespoon vegetable oil
1 small onion, sliced
1 garlic clove, minced
2–4 canned hot green chiles (optional)
5 tablespoons sour cream, plus extra
    to garnish
½ teaspoon ground cumin
hot pepper sauce, to taste
1 tablespoon chopped cilantro

1 Place the beans in a large pan. Add
fresh cold water to cover and the
bay leaf. Bring to a boil, then cover, and
simmer for 30 minutes.

2 Add the sea salt and continue
simmering for about 30 minutes
or until the beans are tender.

3 Drain the cooked beans, reserving
½ cup of the liquid. Let cool slightly.
Discard the bay leaf.

4 Heat the oil in a nonstick frying pan.
Add the onion and garlic and cook
over low heat for 8–10 minutes or
until just softened, stirring occasionally.

5 In a food processor or blender,
combine the beans, onion mixture,
chiles, if using, and the reserved
cooking liquid. Process until the
mixture is a coarse purée.

6 Transfer to a bowl and stir in the
sour cream, cumin, and hot pepper
sauce to taste. Stir in the cilantro, garnish
with sour cream, and serve warm.

VARIATION

To save time, use 2½ 14-ounce cans
beans instead of the dried beans.

Hummus

THIS NUTRITIOUS DIP CAN be served with vegetable crudités or packed into salad-filled pitas, but it is best spread thickly on hot buttered toast. Tahini is a thick, smooth and oily paste made from sesame seeds. It is a classic ingredient in hummus, this Middle-Eastern dip.

Serves 4

INGREDIENTS

14-ounce can chickpeas, drained

2 garlic cloves

2 tablespoons tahini or creamy
    peanut butter

4 tablespoons olive oil

juice of 1 lemon

½ teaspoon cayenne pepper

1 tablespoon sesame seeds

sea salt

Rinse the chickpeas well and place in a food processor or blender with the garlic and a good pinch of sea salt. Process until very finely chopped.

2 Add the tahini or peanut butter, and process until fairly smooth. With the motor still running, slowly pour in the oil and lemon juice.

3 Stir in the cayenne pepper and add more salt to taste. If the mixture is too thick, stir in a little cold water. Transfer the purée to a serving bowl.

4 Heat a small nonstick pan and add the sesame seeds. Cook them for 2–3 minutes, shaking the pan, until they are golden brown in color. Let them cool, then sprinkle them on the purée.

Cannellini Bean Dip

THIS SOFT BEAN DIP or pâté is good
spread on wheat crackers or toasted
English muffins. Alternatively, it can
be served with wedges of tomato
and a crisp green salad.

Serves 4

INGREDIENTS

14-ounce can cannellini beans
grated zest and juice of 1 lemon
2 tablespoons olive oil
1 garlic clove, finely chopped
2 tablespoons chopped fresh parsley
red Tabasco sauce, to taste
salt and ground black pepper
cayenne pepper, to garnish

1 Drain the beans in a sieve and rinse
them well under cold water. Drain
well and transfer to a bowl.

2 Use a potato masher to roughly
purée the beans, then stir in the
lemon zest, juice and olive oil.

3 Stir in the chopped garlic and
parsley. Add Tabasco sauce, salt
and pepper to taste.

4 Spoon the mixture into a small
bowl and dust lightly with cayenne
pepper. Chill until ready to serve.

VARIATION

Canned or cooked butter beans or kidney
beans can also be used for this dip.

Sour Cream Cooler

THIS COOLING DIP MAKES a perfect accompaniment to hot and spicy Mexican dishes. Alternatively, serve it as a snack with the fieriest tortilla chips you can find.

Serves 2

INGREDIENTS

1 small yellow bell pepper

2 small tomatoes

2 tablespoons chopped fresh parsley, plus extra to garnish

⅔ cup sour cream

grated lemon zest, to garnish

1 Halve the pepper lengthwise. With a sharp knife, remove the core and scoop out the seeds, then cut the flesh into tiny dice.

2 Cut the tomatoes in half, then use a teaspoon to scoop out and discard the seeds. Cut the tomato flesh into tiny dice.

3 Stir the pepper and tomato dice and the chopped parsley into the sour cream and mix well.

4 Spoon the dip into a small bowl and chill. Garnish with grated lemon zest and parsley before serving.

VARIATION

Use finely diced avocado or cucumber instead of the pepper or tomato.

Tzatziki

THIS CLASSIC GREEK DIP is a cooling mix of yogurt, cucumber and mint, perfect for a hot summer's day. Serve it with strips of lightly toasted pita bread.

Serves 4

INGREDIENTS

1 mini cucumber

4 scallions

1 garlic clove

scant 1 cup plain yogurt

3 tablespoons chopped fresh mint

salt and ground black pepper

fresh mint sprig, to garnish (optional)

1 Trim the ends from the cucumber, then cut it into ¼-inch dice. Set aside.

2 Trim the scallions and garlic, then chop both very finely.

COOK'S TIP

Choose Greek-style yogurt for this dip— it has a higher fat content than most yogurts, and a deliciously rich, creamy texture.

3 Beat the yogurt until smooth, if necessary, then gently stir in the cucumber, onions, garlic and mint.

4 Add salt and plenty of ground black pepper to taste, then transfer the mixture to a serving bowl. Chill until ready to serve and then garnish with a small mint sprig, if desired.

Red Onion Raita

RAITA IS A TRADITIONAL Indian side dish served as an accompaniment for hot curries. It is also delicious served with poppadums as a dip.

Serves 4

INGREDIENTS

1 teaspoon cumin seeds
1 small garlic clove
1 small green chile
1 large red onion
⅔ cup plain yogurt
2 tablespoons chopped cilantro, plus extra to garnish
½ teaspoon sugar
salt

1 Heat a small frying pan and dry-fry the cumin seeds for 1–2 minutes, until they release their aroma and begin to pop.

VARIATION

For an extra tangy raita stir in 1 tablespoon lemon juice.

2 Lightly crush the seeds in a mortar and pestle or flatten them with the heel of a heavy-bladed knife.

3 Finely chop the garlic. Remove the fiery seeds from the chile and chop the flesh finely, along with the red onion.

4 Place the yogurt in a bowl and add the garlic, chile and red onion, along with the crushed cumin seeds and cilantro. Stir to combine.

5 Add sugar and salt to taste. Spoon the raita into a small bowl and chill until ready to serve. Garnish with extra cilantro before serving.

Saté Dip

A DELICIOUSLY PUNGENT SAUCE which tastes great served with spicy chicken on skewers but is equally good as a dip for crisp vegetables.

Serves 6

INGREDIENTS

scant 1 cup roasted,
  unsalted peanuts
3 tablespoons vegetable oil
1 small onion, roughly chopped
2 garlic cloves, crushed
1 red chile, seeded and chopped
1-inch piece ginger root, peeled
  and chopped
2-inch piece lemongrass,
  roughly chopped
½ teaspoon ground cumin
3 tablespoons chopped cilantro stems
1 tablespoon sesame oil
¾ cup coconut milk
2 tablespoons thick soy sauce (kecap manis)
2 teaspoons lime juice
salt and ground black pepper
lime wedges and chives, to garnish

1 Rub the husks from the peanuts in a clean dish towel.

2 Place the nuts in a food processor or blender with 2 tablespoons vegetable oil, and process into a smooth paste. Transfer to a bowl.

3 Place the next seven ingredients in the food processor or blender and process into a fairly smooth paste.

4 Heat the remaining vegetable oil with the sesame oil in a frying pan and add the onion paste. Cook over low heat for 10–15 minutes, stirring occasionally.

5 Stir in the peanuts, coconut milk, soy sauce and lime juice, and keep stirring while it heats through.

6 Add salt and ground black pepper to taste, then spoon the mixture into small bowls or saucers. Serve warm, garnished with lime wedges and chives.

Spicy Tuna Dip

2 Halve the hard-boiled eggs, remove the yolks and then place in a food processor or blender. Discard the whites or use in another dish.

3 Reserve a few olives for garnishing, then add the rest to the processor or blender together with the remaining ingredients. Process until smooth. Season with pepper to taste.

A PIQUANT DIP, DELICIOUS served with breadsticks—use more oil for a sauce, less for filling hard-boiled eggs, tomatoes or celery sticks.

Serves 6

INGREDIENTS

3¼-ounce can tuna fish in oil
olive oil
3 hard-boiled eggs
¾ cup pitted green olives
2-ounce can anchovy fillets, drained
3 tablespoons capers, drained
2 teaspoons Dijon mustard
ground black pepper
fresh parsley sprigs, to garnish

Drain the oil from the tuna into a small bowl and add olive oil to make 6 tablespoons.

4 Spoon into a bowl and garnish with the reserved olives and the parsley.

COOK'S TIP

Choose a good quality, light olive oil for this dip—richly flavored extra virgin oils may dominate the flavor.

Lemon and Coconut Dhal

A WARM, SPICY DISH, this can be served either as a dip with poppadums or to accompany an Indian main dish.

Serves 8

INGREDIENTS

2 tablespoons sunflower oil
2-inch piece fresh ginger root, finely chopped
1 onion, finely chopped
2 garlic cloves, finely chopped
2 small red chiles, seeded and finely chopped
1 teaspoon cumin seeds
²/₃ cup red lentils
1 cup water
1 tablespoon hot curry paste
scant 1 cup coconut cream
juice of 1 lemon
handful of cilantro leaves
¹/₄ cup sliced almonds
salt and ground black pepper

1 Heat the oil in a large, shallow saucepan. Add the chopped ginger, onion, garlic, chiles and the cumin seeds. Cook for 5 minutes, until softened but not colored.

2 Stir the lentils, water and curry paste into the pan. Bring to a boil, cover and cook gently over low heat for 15–20 minutes, stirring the mixture occasionally, until the lentils are just tender and not yet broken.

3 Stir in all but 2 tablespoons of the coconut cream. Bring to a boil and cook, uncovered, for another 15–20 minutes or until thick and pulpy. Remove from heat, then stir in the lemon juice and the whole cilantro leaves. Add salt and pepper to taste.

VARIATION

Try making this dhal with yellow split peas: they take longer to cook and a little extra water has to be added, but the results are equally tasty.

4 Heat a large pan and cook the almonds for one or two minutes on each side until golden brown. Stir about three-quarters of the toasted almonds into the dhal.

5 Transfer the dhal to a serving bowl and swirl in the remaining coconut cream. Sprinkle the reserved almonds on top and serve warm.

Fonduta

FONTINA IS AN ITALIAN medium-fat cheese with a mild nutty flavor, which melts easily and smoothly. It is a little like Gruyère, which makes a good substitute. This delicious cheese dip needs only some warm ciabatta bread or focaccia, a crisp salad and some robust red wine to complete the meal.

Serves 4

INGREDIENTS
2 cups diced Fontina cheese
1 cup milk
1 tablespoon butter
2 eggs, lightly beaten
ground black pepper

1 Put the cheese in a bowl with the milk and let soak for 2–3 hours. Transfer to a double boiler or a heatproof bowl set over a pan of simmering water.

2 Add the butter and eggs and cook gently, stirring until the cheese has melted to a smooth sauce with the consistency of custard.

3 Remove from heat and season with pepper. Transfer to a serving dish and serve immediately.

COOK'S TIP

Don't overheat the sauce, or the eggs might curdle. Very low heat will produce a smooth sauce.

VARIATION

Pour the Fonduta onto hot pasta or polenta for a really satisfying main dish.

Tahini Yogurt Dip with Sesame seed-coated Falafel

SESAME SEEDS ARE USED to give a crunchy coating to these spicy bean patties. Serve with the tahini yogurt dip and warm pita bread as a light lunch or supper dish.

Serves 4

INGREDIENTS

1⅓ cups dried chickpeas

2 garlic cloves, crushed

1 red chile, seeded and finely sliced

1 teaspoon ground coriander

1 teaspoon ground cumin

1 tablespoon chopped fresh mint

1 tablespoon chopped fresh parsley

2 scallions, finely chopped

1 large egg, beaten

sesame seeds, for coating

sunflower oil, for frying

salt and ground black pepper

For the tahini yogurt dip

2 tablespoons light tahini

scant 1 cup plain yogurt

1 teaspoon cayenne pepper, plus extra for sprinkling

1 tablespoon chopped fresh mint

1 scallion, finely sliced

2 Meanwhile, make the tahini yogurt dip. Mix the tahini, yogurt, cayenne pepper and mint in a small bowl. Sprinkle the scallions and extra cayenne pepper on top and chill until needed.

4 Form the chilled chickpea paste into 12 patties with your hands, then roll each one in the sesame seeds to coat thoroughly.

5 Heat enough oil to cover the bottom of a large frying pan. Fry the falafel, in batches if necessary, for 6 minutes, turning once.

VARIATION

The dip is also great served with vegetable chips.

1 Place the chickpeas in a bowl, cover with cold water and let soak overnight. Drain and rinse the chickpeas, then place in a saucepan and cover with cold water. Bring to a boil and boil rapidly for 10 minutes, then reduce the heat and simmer for 1½–2 hours or until tender.

3 Combine the chickpeas with the garlic, chile, ground spices, herbs, scallions and seasoning, then mix in the egg. Place in a food processor and blend until the mixture forms a coarse paste. If the paste seems too soft, chill it for 30 minutes.

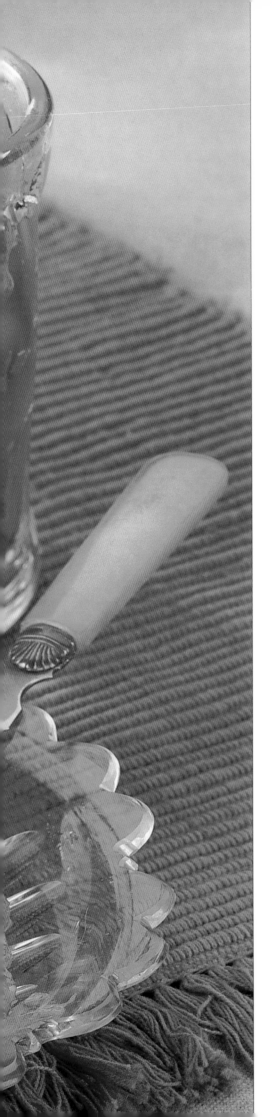

Relishes and Chutneys

It's a myth that preserving is an art—the preparation of a simple chutney or relish is within the reach of any cook, and it's such a worthwhile task. When you line up the jars on your kitchen shelf—and maybe even give a few jars as gifts, you'll feel a real glow of satisfaction.

Once you open the jar, the benefits are even more evident—a spoonful of fruity, spicy chutney or relish can lift the appetite and transform the flavor of the plainest hunk of bread and cheese or meat into a tasty lunch. If your taste is for the unusual, Indian curries are traditionally accompanied by a spoonful of fruity chutney, often made with mangoes, and spiced with chile or ginger.

Almost any cooked meat will benefit from a spicy spoonful of rich chutney on the side—every burger needs its relish, and even a plateful of fresh oysters can be lifted to another level by adding a spoonful of Bloody Mary Relish.

The flavor of most chutneys and relishes improves over time, so, however tempting it may be to eat them immediately, store them carefully for 3–4 weeks before opening the jar to enjoy them at their best.

Classic Quick Recipes

Curried Fruit Chutney

A PIQUANT FRUIT CHUTNEY that is delicious with cold sliced turkey and ham over the Christmas season.

Makes about 2½ pounds

INGREDIENTS

1 cup dried apricots
1⅓ cups dried peaches
1⅓ cups dates, pitted
1⅓ cups raisins
1–2 garlic cloves, crushed
1 cup light brown sugar
1¼ cups malt vinegar
1¼ cups water
1 teaspoon salt
2 teaspoons mild curry powder

VARIATION

For a different flavor and color, pitted prunes can be used instead of the raisins.

1 Put all the ingredients in a large pan, cover and simmer very gently for 10–15 minutes or until tender.

2 Transfer the mixture to a food processor in batches and chop or mince coarsely.

3 Spoon into clean jam jars. Seal the jars and label them. Store in a cool place for 4 weeks before using.

Ginger, Date and Apple Chutney

SERVE THIS RICH, SPICY chutney with cold sliced meats or pies. Make it well ahead to allow time for the warming flavors to mature, and store in airtight jars.

Makes about 3–3½ pounds

INGREDIENTS

1 pound apples
3¼ cups dates, pitted
1 cup dried apricots
4 ounces crystallized ginger, chopped
1–2 garlic cloves, crushed
1⅓ cups golden raisins
1 cup light brown sugar
1 teaspoon salt
1¼ cups malt vinegar

VARIATION

If you prefer, drained pieces of preserved stem ginger in syrup can be used instead of the crystallized ginger.

1 Peel, core and chop the apples into small chunks. Roughly chop the dates and apricots.

2 Put all the fruit together in a large with all the remaining ingredients. Cover and simmer gently for 10–15 minutes or until the fruit is tender and the liquid is well reduced.

3 Spoon into clean jam jars. Seal the jars and label them. Store in a cool place for 4 weeks before using.

Anchovy and Parsley Relish

ANCHOVIES AND PARSLEY make a flavorful relish to serve as a topping for fresh vegetables. Serve these fresh-tasting nibbles as an appetizer to a rich meal, or with drinks.

Makes about 8 ounces

INGREDIENTS

2 ounces flat-leaf parsley
½ cup black olives, pitted
½ cup sun-dried tomatoes
4 canned anchovy fillets, drained
2 ounces red onion, finely chopped
1 ounce small pickled capers, rinsed
1 garlic clove, finely chopped
1 tablespoon olive oil
juice of ½ lime
¼ teaspoon ground black pepper
a selection of cherry tomatoes, radishes, celery and cucumber, to serve

1 Coarsely chop the parsley, black olives, sun-dried tomatoes and anchovy fillets and mix in a bowl with the onion, capers, garlic, olive oil, lime juice and black pepper.

2 Halve the cherry tomatoes and radishes, chop the celery into bite-size chunks and cut the cucumber into ½-inch slices. Top each of the prepared vegetables with a generous amount of relish and serve immediately.

Spiced Cranberry and Orange Relish

THIS COLORFUL, FESTIVE RELISH is excellent served with roast turkey, goose or duck.

Makes about 1 pound

INGREDIENTS

2 cups fresh cranberries
1 onion, finely chopped
⅔ cup port
generous ½ cup sugar
finely grated zest and juice of 1 orange
½ teaspoon English mustard powder
¼ teaspoon ground ginger
¼ teaspoon ground cinnamon
1 teaspoon cornstarch
scant ½ cup raisins

COOK'S TIP

Frozen cranberries can be used instead of fresh—simply add them straight from the freezer.

1 Put the cranberries, onion, port and sugar in a pan. Cook the mixture gently for 10 minutes or until tender.

2 Mix the orange juice, mustard powder, ginger, cinnamon and cornstarch. Stir them into the cranberries.

3 Add the raisins and orange zest. Let thicken over the heat, stirring, and then simmer for 2 minutes. Cool, cover and chill ready for serving.

Pickled Peach and Chili Chutney

THIS IS A REALLY SPICY, rich chutney that is great served with cold roast meats such as ham, pork or turkey. It is also good with a strong farmhouse Cheddar cheese.

Makes about 1 pound

INGREDIENTS

2 cups cider vinegar

1¼ cups light brown sugar

1½ cups pitted and finely chopped
    dried dates

1 teaspoon ground allspice

1 teaspoon ground mace

1 pound ripe peaches, pitted

3 onions, thinly sliced

4 fresh red chiles, seeded and
    finely chopped

4 garlic cloves, crushed

2-inch piece of fresh ginger root,
    finely grated

1 teaspoon salt

1 Place the vinegar, sugar, chopped dates and spices in a large, heavy saucepan and bring to a boil, stirring occasionally.

2 Cut the peaches into small chunks. Add to the pan with all the remaining ingredients and return the mixture to a boil. Lower the heat and simmer for 40–50 minutes or until thick. Stir frequently to prevent the mixture from burning on the bottom of the saucepan.

3 Spoon the chutney into clean, sterilized jars and seal. When cold, store the jars in the refrigerator and use within 2 months.

COOK'S TIP

To test the consistency of the finished chutney before bottling, spoon a little of the mixture onto a plate: the chutney is ready once it holds its shape.

Nectarine Relish

THIS SWEET AND TANGY fruit relish goes very well with hot roast meats and game birds, such as guinea fowl, pheasant and pork. Make it while nectarines are plentiful and keep tightly covered in the refrigerator to serve at a later date.

Makes about 1 pound

INGREDIENTS

3 tablespoons olive oil

2 Spanish onions, thinly sliced

1 fresh green chile, seeded and
    finely chopped

1 teaspoon finely chopped fresh rosemary

2 bay leaves

1 pound nectarines, pitted and diced

1 cup raisins

2 teaspoons crushed coriander seeds

1½ cups sugar

scant 1 cup red wine vinegar

1 Heat the oil in a large, heavy saucepan. Add the sliced onions, chopped chile and rosemary, and the bay leaves. Cook, stirring frequently, for 15–20 minutes or until the onions are soft but not browned.

2 Add all the remaining ingredients and bring to a boil slowly, stirring often. Lower the heat and simmer for 1 hour or until the relish is thick and sticky, stirring occasionally.

3 Remove and discard the bay leaves. Spoon into sterilized jars, and seal. Cool, then chill. The relish will keep in the refrigerator for up to 5 months.

COOK'S TIP

Jars of this relish make a welcome gift. Add a colorful tag reminding the recipient to keep it in the refrigerator.

Piquant Pineapple Relish

THIS FRUITY SWEET-AND-SOUR relish is excellent served with chicken, ham or bacon.

Serves 4

INGREDIENTS

14-ounce can crushed pineapple in
    natural juice
2 tablespoons light brown sugar
2 tablespoons wine vinegar
1 garlic clove, finely chopped
4 scallions, finely chopped
2 red chiles, seeded and chopped
10 fresh basil leaves, finely shredded
salt and ground black pepper

1 Drain the pineapple and reserve 4 tablespoons of the juice.

2 Place the juice in a small saucepan with the sugar and vinegar, then heat gently, stirring frequently, until the sugar dissolves. Remove the pan from heat and season with salt and pepper to taste.

3 Place the pineapple, garlic, scallions and chiles in a bowl. Mix well and stir in the juice. Let cool for 5 minutes, then stir in the basil and serve.

VARIATION

This relish tastes extra special when made with fresh pineapple.

Papaya and Lemon Relish

THIS CHUNKY RELISH IS best made with a firm, unripe papaya. Leave for a week before eating to let all the flavors mellow. Store unopened jars in a cool place, away from sunlight. Serve with roast meats or with a robust cheese and crackers.

Makes about 1 pound

INGREDIENTS

1 large unripe papaya
1 onion, thinly sliced
⅓ cup raisins
1 cup red wine vinegar
juice of 2 lemons
⅔ cup elderflower cordial
¾ cup sugar
1 cinnamon stick
1 fresh bay leaf
½ teaspoon hot paprika
½ teaspoon salt

1 Peel the papaya and cut lengthwise in half. Remove the seeds with a teaspoon. Use a sharp knife to cut the flesh into small chunks and place them in a saucepan. Add the onion slices and raisins, then stir in the red wine vinegar.

2 Bring the liquid to a boil, then immediately lower the heat and let simmer for 10 minutes.

COOK'S TIP

The seeds of papaya are often discarded when the ripe fruit is used, but they have a peppery taste and make a delicious addition to a salad dressing.

3 Add all the remaining ingredients to the saucepan and bring to a boil, stirring all the time. Check that all the sugar has dissolved, then lower the heat and simmer for 50–60 minutes or until the relish is thick and syrupy.

4 Remove and discard the bay leaf. Ladle the relish into hot, sterilized jars. Seal and label, and store in a cool, dark place for 1 week before using. Keep the relish chilled after opening.

Spicy Corn Relish

SERVE THIS SIMPLE SPICY relish with bowls of Red Onion Raita, Sweet Mango Relish and a plateful of crisp onion bhajis for a fabulous Indian-style appetizer.

Serves 4

INGREDIENTS

2 tablespoons vegetable oil
1 large onion, chopped
1 red chile, seeded and chopped
2 garlic cloves, chopped
1 teaspoon black mustard seeds
2 teaspoons hot curry powder
11¼-ounce can corn, drained
grated zest and juice of 1 lime
3 tablespoons chopped cilantro
salt and ground black pepper

1 Heat the oil in a large frying pan and cook the onion, chile and garlic over high heat for 5 minutes, until the onions are just beginning to brown.

COOK'S TIP

Use frozen rather than canned corn, as the kernels are plump and moist.

2 Stir in the mustard seeds and curry powder, then cook for 2 more minutes, stirring, until the seeds start to splutter and the onions are browned.

3 Remove the fried onion and spice mixture from heat and let cool completely. Transfer the mixture to a glass bowl.

4 Add the drained corn to the bowl containing the onion mixture and stir to mix.

5 Add the lime zest and juice, cilantro and seasoning. Mix well, then cover and serve at room temperature.

Sweet Mango Relish

STIR A SPOONFUL OF this relish into soups and stews for added flavor or serve it with a wedge of Cheddar cheese and chunks of crusty bread.

Makes 3 cups

INGREDIENTS

2 large mangoes

1 apple, peeled and chopped

2 shallots, chopped

1½-inch piece fresh ginger root, chopped

2 garlic cloves, crushed

⅔ cup small golden raisins

2 star anise

1 teaspoon ground cinnamon

½ teaspoon dried chile flakes

½ teaspoon salt

¾ cup cider vinegar

generous ½ cup light brown sugar

1 One at a time, hold the mangoes upright on a cutting board and use a large knife to slice the flesh off each side of the large, flat pit.

2 Using a smaller knife, carefully trim off any flesh still clinging to the top and bottom of the pit.

3 Score the flesh of the mango halves deeply, taking care to avoid cutting through the skin: make parallel incisions about ½ inch apart, then turn and cut parallel lines in the opposite direction.

4 Carefully turn the skin inside out so that the mango flesh stands out like hedgehog spikes. Slice the dice from the skin.

5 Place the diced mango, chopped apple, shallots, ginger, garlic and golden raisins in a large, heavy saucepan. Add the star anise, cinnamon, chile, salt, vinegar and sugar.

6 Bring to a boil, stirring continuously, until the sugar has dissolved. Reduce the heat and simmer gently for another 4 minutes, stirring occasionally, until the chutney has reduced and thickened.

7 Let the relish cool for about 5 minutes, then ladle it into warm, sterilized jars. Cool completely, cover and label. The relish may be stored in the refrigerator for up to 2 months. Keep the relish chilled after opening.

VARIATION

Select alternative spices according to your own taste: for example, you can add juniper berries or cumin seeds instead of the star anise.

Chili Relish

THIS SPICY RELISH will keep for at least a week in the refrigerator. Serve it with sausages or with burgers in sesame seed buns.

Serves 8

INGREDIENTS

6 tomatoes
2 tablespoons olive oil
1 onion, roughly chopped
1 red bell pepper, seeded and chopped
2 garlic cloves, chopped
1 teaspoon ground cinnamon
1 teaspoon chile flakes
1 teaspoon ground ginger
1 teaspoon salt
½ teaspoon ground black pepper
6 tablespoons light brown sugar
5 tablespoons cider vinegar
handful of fresh basil leaves, chopped

1 Skewer each of the tomatoes in turn on a metal fork and hold in a gas flame for 1–2 minutes, turning, until the skin splits and wrinkles.

2 Slip off the tomato skins, then roughly chop the flesh.

3 Heat the olive oil in a saucepan. Add the chopped onion, red pepper and garlic to the pan.

4 Cook gently for 5–8 minutes or until the pepper is softened. Add the chopped tomatoes, cover and cook for 5 minutes, until the tomatoes release their juices.

5 Stir in the cinnamon, chile flakes, ginger, salt, pepper, sugar and vinegar. Bring gently to a boil, stirring, until the sugar dissolves.

6 Simmer, uncovered, for 20 minutes or until the mixture is pulpy. Stir in the basil leaves and check the seasoning.

7 Let cool completely, then transfer to a glass jar or a plastic container with a tightly fitting lid. Store, covered, in the refrigerator.

COOK'S TIP

This relish thickens slightly on cooling, so do not worry if the mixture seems a little wet at the end of step 6.

VARIATION

Replace the fresh garlic with smoked garlic for a really smoky, barbecue flavor.

Bloody Mary Relish

SERVE THIS PERFECT PARTY relish with sticks of crunchy cucumber or, on a really special occasion, with freshly shucked oysters.

Serves 2

INGREDIENTS

4 ripe tomatoes
1 celery stalk
1 garlic clove
2 scallions
3 tablespoons tomato juice
Worcestershire sauce, to taste
red Tabasco sauce, to taste
2 teaspoons horseradish sauce
1 tablespoon vodka
juice of 1 lemon
salt and ground black pepper

1 Halve the tomatoes, celery and garlic. Trim the scallions.

2 Process the vegetables in a food processor or blender until very finely chopped. Transfer to a bowl.

3 Stir in the tomato juice and add a few drops of Worcestershire sauce and Tabasco to taste.

4 Stir in the horseradish sauce, vodka and lemon juice. Season with salt and ground black pepper, to taste.

VARIATION

In the food processor or blender add 1–2 fresh, seeded, red chiles with the tomatoes, celery and garlic instead of adding Tabasco sauce.

Tart Tomato Relish

THE WHOLE LIME used in this recipe adds a pleasantly sour aftertaste. This is delicious served with grilled or roast pork or lamb.

Serves 4

INGREDIENTS

1 lime

1 pound cherry tomatoes

½ cup dark brown sugar

7 tablespoons white wine vinegar

1 teaspoon salt

2 pieces stem ginger, chopped

1 Slice the whole lime thinly, then chop it into small pieces; do not remove the zest.

VARIATION

If preferred, use ordinary tomatoes, roughly chopped, instead of the cherry tomatoes used here.

2 Place the whole tomatoes, sugar, vinegar, salt, ginger and lime together in a saucepan.

3 Bring to a boil, stirring until the sugar dissolves, then simmer rapidly for 45 minutes. Stir regularly until the liquid has evaporated and the relish is thickened and pulpy.

4 Let the relish cool for about 5 minutes, then spoon it into clean jars. Cool completely, cover and store in the refrigerator for up to 1 month.

Caramelized Onion Relish

SLOW, GENTLE COOKING reduces the onions to a soft, caramelized golden brown relish in this recipe. This relish adds a sweet flavor to all kinds of meat and makes an idea accompaniment to flans and quiches.

Serves 4

INGREDIENTS

3 large onions
¼ cup butter
2 tablespoons olive oil
2 tablespoons light brown sugar
2 tablespoons pickled capers
2 tablespoons chopped fresh parsley
salt and ground black pepper

1 Peel the onions and cut them in half vertically through the core, then slice them thinly.

2 Heat the butter and oil together in a large, heavy saucepan. Add the sliced onions and sugar and cook very gently for about 30 minutes over low heat, stirring occasionally, until the onions are reduced to a soft rich-brown mixture.

3 Roughly chop the capers and stir into the browned onion mixture. Let cool completely and transfer to a bowl.

4 Stir in the chopped parsley and add salt and freshly ground black pepper to taste. Cover and chill until ready to serve.

COOK'S TIP

Choose a heavy pan to cook the relish in, to get an evenly browned mixture without the risk of burning.

VARIATION

Try making this recipe with red onions or shallots for a subtle variation in flavor.

Red Onion Marmalade

THIS IS A RICH and delicious marmalade, and makes a particularly good accompaniment to grilled salmon.

Serves 4

INGREDIENTS

5 red onions

¼ cup butter

¾ cup red wine vinegar

¼ cup crème de cassis

¼ cup grenadine

¼ cup red wine

salt and ground black pepper

1 Remove the skins from the red onions and slice them finely.

2 Melt the butter in a large, heavy saucepan and add the sliced onions. Sauté the onions for 5 minutes, or until golden brown.

3 Stir in the wine vinegar, crème de cassis, grenadine and wine and continue to cook for about 10 minutes or until the liquid has almost entirely evaporated and the onions are glazed. Season well with salt and freshly ground black pepper.

COOK'S TIP

If serving this marmalade with salmon, try to find pieces that are at least 1 inch thick. Brush the fish with olive oil, season with salt and ground black pepper, and cook over medium heat for 6–8 minutes, turning once during cooking.

Apple and Red Onion Marmalade

THIS MARMALADE CHUTNEY is good enough to eat on its own. Serve it with good quality pork sausages for thoroughly modern hot dogs, or in a ham sandwich instead of mustard.

Makes about 1 pound

INGREDIENTS

4 tablespoons extra virgin olive oil
2 pounds red onions, thinly sliced
6 tablespoons sugar
2 apples
6 tablespoons cider vinegar

1 Heat the oil in a large, heavy saucepan and add the onions.

2 Stir in the sugar and let cook, uncovered, over medium heat for about 40 minutes, stirring occasionally, until the onions have softened.

3 Peel, core and grate the apples. Add them to the pan with the vinegar and continue to cook for 20 minutes or until the chutney is thick and sticky. Spoon into sterilized jars and cover.

4 When cool, label and store in the refrigerator for up to 1 month.

VARIATION

If desired, add a cinnamon stick to the pan during cooking to impart a mild, sweet spicy flavor. Remove the stick before bottling the marmalade chutney in sterilized jars.

Old-fashioned Pickles

THESE SIMPLE, OLD-FASHIONED pickles are quite delicious with cold meats or cheese, with a hunk of fresh crusty bread and butter on the side.

Makes about 3–3½ pounds

INGREDIENTS

2 pounds cucumbers, scrubbed and cut in
   ¼-inch slices
4 onions, very thinly sliced
2 tablespoons salt
1½ cups cider vinegar
generous 1½ cups sugar
2 tablespoons mustard seeds
2 tablespoons celery seeds
¼ teaspoon turmeric
¼ teaspoon cayenne

COOK'S TIP

Avoid using metal lids or seals, as these may react with the acid in the pickle.

1 Put the sliced cucumbers and onions in a large bowl and sprinkle with the salt. Mix well. Cover loosely and let stand for 3 hours.

2 Drain the vegetables. Rinse well under cold running water and then drain again.

3 Prepare some heatproof glass jars (such as preserving jars). Wash them well in warm soapy water and rinse thoroughly in clean warm water.

4 Place the jars on a baking sheet in the oven at 300°F for 30 minutes to sterilize. Keep the jars hot until ready to use.

5 Combine the remaining ingredients in a large, non-reactive saucepan and bring to a boil. Add the drained cucumbers and onions. Reduce the heat and simmer for 2–3 minutes. Do not boil, or the pickles will be limp.

6 Spoon the hot vegetables into the hot jars. Add enough of the liquid to come to ½ inch from the top. Carefully wipe the jars with a clean damp cloth.

7 To seal, cover the surface of the pickles with a waxed disc, waxed side down, then put on the jar lids. The pickles should be sealed immediately. If the lid does not have a ring gasket, first cover the top of the jar with a plastic wrap or cellophane cover then screw the plastic top down tightly. Set in a cool dark place for at least 4 weeks.

Christmas Chutney

THIS SAVORY MIXTURE OF spices and dried fruit takes its inspiration from mincemeat and makes a delicious traditional addition to a holiday buffet. Serve with cold meats.

Makes about 2¼–3½ pounds

INGREDIENTS

1 pound cooking apples, peeled, cored and chopped

3⅓ cups luxury mixed dried fruit

grated zest of 1 orange

2 tablespoons allspice

⅔ cup cider vinegar

1½ cups light brown sugar

1 Place the chopped apples, dried fruit and grated orange zest in a large, heavy saucepan. Stir in the allspice, cider vinegar and sugar. Heat the ingredients gently, stirring until all the sugar has dissolved.

2 Bring to a boil, then lower the heat and simmer the mixture for 40–45 minutes, stirring occasionally, until thick.

3 Ladle into warm, sterilized jars, cover and seal. Keep for 1 month before using.

COOK'S TIPS

• Watch the chutney carefully toward the end of the cooking time, as it has a tendency to stick to the bottom of the pan. Stir frequently at this stage.

• Store jars in the refrigerator after opening.

Fig and Date Chutney

THIS RECIPE IS USUALLY made with dried figs and dates, but fresh fruit provides a superb flavor and texture.

Makes about 1 pound

INGREDIENTS

1 orange

5 large fresh figs, coarsely chopped

2½ cups fresh dates, peeled, pitted and chopped

2 onions, chopped

2-inch piece of fresh ginger root, peeled and finely grated

1 teaspoon dried crushed chiles

generous 1½ cups sugar

1¼ cups spiced preserving vinegar

½ teaspoon salt

COOK'S TIP

Figs are in season for only a short time, so buy when you see them in the shops.

1 Finely grate the zest of the orange, then cut off the remaining pith.

VARIATION

If you would rather use dried figs and dates to make the chutney, you will need to increase the amount of preserving vinegar to a scant 2 cups. Remove the pits from the dates and then coarsely chop both the figs and the dates.

2 Place the orange segments in a large, heavy saucepan with the chopped figs and dates. Add the zest, then stir in the remaining ingredients. Bring to a boil, stirring until the sugar has dissolved, then lower the heat and simmer gently for 1 hour or until thickened and pulpy, stirring frequently.

3 Spoon into hot sterilized jars. Seal while the chutney is still hot and label when cold. Store in a cool dark place for 1 week before using. Keep opened jars in the refrigerator.

Fresh Pineapple and Mint Chutney

THIS REFRESHING, LIGHT FRUIT chutney has a fresh flavor; it is good with rich meat dishes, particularly lamb or pork.

Makes about 2¼ pounds

INGREDIENTS
1 cup raspberry vinegar
1 cup dry white wine
1 small pineapple, peeled and chopped
2 medium-size oranges, peeled
   and chopped
2 apples, peeled and chopped
1 red bell pepper, seeded and diced
1½ onions, finely chopped
4 tablespoons honey
pinch of salt
1 whole clove
4 black peppercorns
2 tablespoons chopped fresh mint

1 In a large saucepan, combine the raspberry vinegar and white wine, and bring to a boil. Boil for 3 minutes.

2 Add the remaining ingredients, except the mint, and stir to blend. Simmer gently for about 30 minutes, stirring occasionally.

3 Transfer to a strainer set over a bowl and drain, pressing down to extract the liquid. Remove and discard the clove and peppercorns. Set the fruit mixture aside.

4 Return the strained juice to the pan and boil until reduced by two-thirds. Pour onto the fruit mixture.

5 Stir in the mint. Let stand for 6–8 hours before serving.

COOK'S TIP

The chutney will keep for about 1 week in the refrigerator. If you can get pineapple mint, this adds a delightful fresh pineapple scent to the finished chutney.

Mango Chutney

THIS CLASSIC CHUTNEY IS frequently
served with curries and Indian
poppadums, but it is also delicious
with baked ham.

Makes about 1 pound

INGREDIENTS

3 firm green mangoes
⅔ cup cider vinegar
generous ½ cup light brown sugar
1 small red finger chile or jalapeño chile, split
*1-inch piece of fresh ginger root, peeled and
    finely chopped*
1 garlic clove, finely chopped
5 cardamom pods, bruised
½ teaspoon coriander seeds, crushed
1 bay leaf
½ teaspoon salt

1 Peel the mangoes and cut the flesh
off the pit. Slice them lengthwise,
then cut into small chunks or wedges.

COOK'S TIP

*Green, underripe mangoes have quite a
sharp, tangy flavor, quite unlike the
fragrant sweetness of ripe ones, but ideal
for chutneys and relishes to serve with
savory foods.*

2 Place these in a large saucepan, add
the vinegar and cover. Cook over
low heat for 10 minutes.

3 Stir in the sugar, chile, ginger, garlic,
bruised cardamom pods and
coriander seeds. Add the bay leaf and
salt. Bring to a boil slowly, stirring the
mixture often.

4 Lower the heat and simmer,
uncovered, for 30 minutes, until
the mixture is thick and syrupy. Remove
the cardamom pods and remove and
discard the bay leaf.

5 Ladle into hot, sterilized jars. Let
cool, then seal and label. Store in a
cool, dark place for 1 week before
eating. Keep chilled after opening.

Roasted Red Bell Pepper and Chili Jelly

THE HINT OF CHILE in this glowing red jelly makes it ideal for spicing up hot or cold roast meat. The jelly is also good stirred into sauces.

Makes about 2 pounds

INGREDIENTS

8 red bell peppers, quartered and seeded

4 fresh red chiles, halved and seeded

1 onion, roughly chopped

2 garlic cloves, roughly chopped

1 cup water

1 cup white wine vinegar

1½ teaspoons salt

2¼ cups sugar

⅓-ounce envelope powdered pectin (about 1½ tablespoons)

COOK'S TIP

If you can find it, use preserving sugar, which produces less scum.

1 Place the peppers, skin side up, on a rack in a broiler pan. Broil until the skins blister and blacken. Place in a plastic bag until cool enough to handle, then remove the skins.

2 Purée the red peppers with the chiles, onion, garlic and water in a food processor or blender. Press the purée through a nylon sieve set over a bowl, pressing hard with a wooden spoon, to extract as much juice as possible. There should be roughly 3 cups.

3 Scrape the purée into a large, stainless steel pan. Add the vinegar and salt. In a bowl, mix the sugar and pectin, then stir into the liquid.

4 Heat gently until both the sugar and pectin have dissolved, then bring to a full rolling boil. Boil, stirring frequently, for exactly 4 minutes.

5 Remove the jelly from heat and pour into warm, sterilized jars. Let cool and set, then cover. Keep opened jars in the refrigerator.

Dressings
and
Marinades

The primary function of dressings and marinades is to add or balance flavor, and this can make all the difference to even the simplest foods. Both are usually based on a mix of oil and an acidic ingredient such as vinegar or fruit juice, with aromatic additions such as herbs, garlic or spices for a more individual flavor.

Dressings are used to moisten foods, add variety and lift the flavor of any type of salad, from simple green leaves to substantial main course salads. They are also of benefit to other foods, such as lightly cooked spears of asparagus, bok choy and crudités.

Marinades are used not only to add flavor to foods but can also tenderize meats and add moisture to dry foods, either before cooking or as a baste during cooking. A light summer herb marinade makes a world of difference to the flavor of a simple piece of fish or meat, and try a peppered citrus marinade to add a delicious zip to meaty-textured monkfish. The tenderizing effect, caused by the acid content in marinades, is particularly beneficial for tough meats or poultry. A yogurt marinade has a tenderizing effect, too, with the added benefit of forming a deliciously tangy crust on the outside of grilled food.

Avocado Dressing with Crudités

THIS CREAMY-TEXTURED DRESSING is actually quite light and also makes a good dressing for tomato salads.

Makes a scant 2 cups

INGREDIENTS

2 tablespoons wine vinegar

½ teaspoon salt, or to taste

¾ teaspoon white pepper

½ red onion, coarsely chopped

3 tablespoons olive oil

1 large ripe avocado, halved and pitted

1 tablespoon fresh lemon juice

3 tablespoons plain yogurt

3 tablespoons water, or as needed

2 tablespoons chopped cilantro

raw or briefly cooked cold vegetables,
*   to serve*

1 In a bowl, combine the vinegar and salt and stir with a fork to dissolve. Stir in the pepper, chopped red onion, and olive oil.

2 Scoop the avocado flesh into a food processor or blender. Add the lemon juice and onion dressing and process just to blend.

3 Add the yogurt and water and process until the mixture is smooth. If desired, add more water to thin. Taste and adjust the seasoning according to taste.

4 Spoon the mixture into a bowl. Stir in the cilantro. Serve immediately with the raw or briefly cooked cold vegetables.

COOK'S TIP

This versatile dressing need not be limited to serving with crudités and salads. Serve it as a sauce with grilled chicken or fish, or use it on sandwiches instead of mayonnaise or mustard, or to provide a cool contrast to any sort of spicy food.

Lime Dressing with Bok Choy

FOR THIS THAI RECIPE, the lime dressing is traditionally made using fish sauce, but vegetarians could use vinegar. Beware, this is a fiery dish!

Serves 4

INGREDIENTS

6 scallions

2 bok choy

2 tablespoons oil

3 fresh red chiles, cut into thin strips

4 garlic cloves, thinly sliced

1 tablespoon crushed peanuts

salt

For the lime dressing

1–2 tablespoons fish sauce

2 tablespoons lime juice

1 cup coconut milk

COOK'S TIP

Coconut milk is available in cans. Alternatively, creamed coconut is available in packages. To use creamed coconut, place about 4 ounces in a bowl and pour in 1 cup boiling water. Stir well until dissolved.

1 To make the dressing, blend together the fish sauce and lime juice, and then stir in the coconut milk.

2 Cut the scallions diagonally into slices, including all but the tips of the green parts. Keep the white parts separate from the green.

3 Using a large, sharp knife, cut the bok choy into very fine shreds.

4 Heat the oil in a wok and stir-fry the chiles for 2–3 minutes or until crisp. Transfer to a plate using a slotted spoon. Stir-fry the garlic for 30–60 seconds or until golden brown, and transfer to the plate with the chiles.

5 Stir-fry the white parts of the scallions for 2–3 minutes and then add the green parts and stir-fry for another 1 minute. Add to the plate with the chiles and garlic.

6 Bring a large pan of salted water to a boil and add the shredded bok choy. Stir twice and then drain in a sieve or colander immediately.

7 Place the warmed bok choy in a large bowl, add the dressing and stir well.

8 Spoon into a large serving bowl and sprinkle with the crushed peanuts and the stir-fried chili mixture. Serve either warm or cold, as an accompaniment to rice dishes.

Creamy Raspberry Dressing with Asparagus

RASPBERRY VINEGAR gives this quick dressing a refreshing, tangy fruit flavor—an ideal accompaniment to asparagus.

Serves 4

INGREDIENTS

1½ pounds thin asparagus spears
1½ cups fresh raspberries,
   to garnish

For the creamy raspberry dressing

2 tablespoons raspberry vinegar
½ teaspoon salt
1 teaspoon Dijon-style mustard
4 tablespoons crème fraîche or
   plain yogurt
ground white pepper

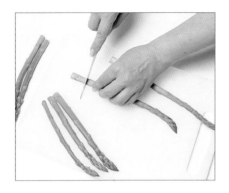

Fill a saucepan with water about 4 inches deep and bring to a boil. Trim the tough ends of the asparagus spears.

COOK'S TIP

Cook the asparagus and make the sauce in advance, then chill in the refrigerator until needed. Serve cold.

2 Tie the asparagus spears into two bundles. Lower the bundles into the boiling water and cook for 3–5 minutes, until just tender.

3 Remove the asparagus and immerse it in cold water to stop the cooking. Drain and untie the bundles. Pat dry. Chill for 1 hour.

4 To make the dressing, mix the vinegar and salt in a bowl and stir with a fork until dissolved. Stir in the mustard, crème fraîche or yogurt. Add pepper to taste. Place the asparagus on individual plates and drizzle the dressing across the middle of the spears. Garnish with fresh raspberries.

Cilantro Dressing with Chicken Salad

SERVE THIS SALAD WARM to make the most of the wonderful flavor of grilled chicken basted with a marinade of cilantro, sesame and mustard, and finished with a matching dressing.

Serves 6

INGREDIENTS

4 medium boneless chicken
   breasts, skinned
8 ounces snow peas
2 heads decorative lettuce such as lollo
   rosso or feuille de chêne
3 carrots, cut into matchsticks
2¼ cups button
   mushrooms, sliced
6 strips bacon, fried and chopped
1 tablespoon chopped cilantro,
   to garnish

For the cilantro dressing
½ cup lemon juice
2 tablespoons whole-grain mustard
1 cup olive oil
5 tablespoons sesame oil
1 teaspoon coriander seeds, crushed

1 Mix all the dressing ingredients in a bowl. Place the chicken breasts in a dish and pour over half the dressing. Marinate overnight in the refrigerator. Refrigerate the remaining dressing.

2 Cook the snow peas for about 2 minutes in boiling water, then refresh in cold water.

3 Tear the lettuces into small pieces and mix with all the other salad ingredients and the bacon. Arrange in individual bowls.

4 Cook the chicken breasts on a medium grill for 10–15 minutes, basting with the marinade and turning once, until cooked through.

COOK'S TIP

If you have any spare dressing left over, store it in a screw-topped jar in the refrigerator for up to 4 days. Use the dressing for drizzling on other salads.

5 Slice the chicken on the diagonal into thin pieces. Divide among the bowls of salad and add some of the dressing to each dish. Combine quickly and sprinkle some cilantro on each bowl.

Ginger and Lime Marinade for Shrimp

THIS FRAGRANT MARINADE will guarantee a mouthwatering aroma from the grill, and is as delicious with chicken or pork as it is with shrimp.

Serves 4

INGREDIENTS

8 ounces peeled tiger shrimp

¹/₃ cucumber

1 tablespoon sunflower oil

1 tablespoon sesame seed oil

6 ounces snow peas, trimmed

4 scallions, diagonally sliced

2 tablespoons chopped cilantro,
  to garnish

For the ginger and lime marinade

1 tablespoon clear honey

1 tablespoon light soy sauce

1 tablespoon dry sherry

2 garlic cloves, crushed

small piece of fresh ginger root, peeled and
  finely chopped

juice of 1 lime

1 Mix the marinade ingredients, add the shrimp and let marinate for 1-2 hours.

2 Prepare the cucumber. Slice it in half lengthwise, scoop out the seeds, then slice each half neatly into crescents. Set aside.

3 Heat both oils in a large, heavy frying pan or wok. Drain the shrimp (reserving the marinade) and stir-fry over high heat for 4 minutes or until they begin to turn pink. Add the snow peas and the cucumber and stir-fry for 2 more minutes.

4 Stir in the reserved marinade, heat through, then stir in the scallions and sprinkle with chopped cilantro to garnish.

VARIATION

This marinade is also a good one to use with larger pieces of fish for grilling, such as salmon, trout or tuna.

Peppered Citrus Marinade for Monkfish

MONKFISH IS A FIRM, meaty fish that cooks well on the grill. Serve with a green salad.

Serves 4

INGREDIENTS

2 monkfish tails, about 12 ounces each

1 lime

1 lemon

2 oranges

handful of fresh thyme sprigs

2 tablespoons olive oil

1 tablespoon mixed peppercorns, roughly crushed

salt and ground black pepper

1 Using a sharp kitchen knife, remove any skin from the monkfish tails. Cut the fish carefully down one side of the backbone, sliding the knife between the bone and flesh, to remove the fillet on one side.

2 Turn the fish and repeat on the other side, to remove the second fillet. Repeat on the second tail. Place the four fillets flat on a cutting board.

3 Cut two slices from each of the citrus fruits and arrange them over two of the fillets.

4 Add a few sprigs of fresh thyme, and sprinkle with plenty of salt and ground black pepper. Finely grate the zest from the remaining fruit and sprinkle it on the fish.

5 Lay the other two fillets on top and tie them firmly at intervals.

6 Squeeze the juice from the citrus fruits and mix it with the olive oil and more salt and pepper. Spoon onto the fish. Cover with plastic wrap and let marinate in the refrigerator for about 1 hour, turning the fish occasionally and spooning the marinade on it.

7 Drain the monkfish, reserving the marinade, and sprinkle with the crushed peppercorns. Cook over medium-hot grill for 15–20 minutes, basting with the marinade.

VARIATION

If you prefer, remove the peel from the fruit before placing between the fillets.

Orange and Green Peppercorn Marinade for Bass

THIS IS AN EXCELLENT light marinade for using with whole fish. The cooked fish, in the lovely soft-colored marinade, needs only a fresh herb sprig as garnish. Other suitable fish for this recipe are salmon trout or sea bream.

Serves 4

INGREDIENTS

1 medium whole sea bass, cleaned

For the peppercorn marinade

1 red onion

2 small oranges

6 tablespoons light olive oil

2 tablespoons cider vinegar

2 tablespoons green peppercorns in brine, drained

2 tablespoons chopped fresh parsley

salt and sugar, to taste

1 With a sharp knife, slash the sea bass three or four times on both sides.

2 Line an ovenproof dish with foil. Peel and slice the onion and oranges. Place half in the bottom of the dish, place the fish on top, and cover with the remaining onion and orange.

3 Mix the remaining marinade ingredients and pour onto the fish. Cover and stand for 4 hours, occasionally spooning the marinade on the top.

4 Preheat the oven to 350°F. Fold up the foil over the fish and seal loosely. Bake for 15 minutes per 1 pound, plus 15 more minutes. Serve with the juices.

Summer Herb Marinade for Salmon

MAKE USE OF SUMMER herbs in this marinade, which can also be used with veal, chicken, pork or lamb.

Serves 4

INGREDIENTS

4 salmon steaks or fillets, about 6 ounces each

For the herb marinade
large handful of fresh herb sprigs, e.g.
   chervil, thyme, parsley, sage, chives,
   rosemary, oregano
6 tablespoons olive oil
3 tablespoons tarragon vinegar
1 garlic clove, crushed
2 scallions, chopped
salt and ground black pepper

1 Discard any coarse stems or damaged leaves from the herbs, then chop them very finely.

2 Add the chopped herbs to the remaining marinade ingredients in a large bowl. Stir to mix thoroughly.

3 Place the salmon in the bowl and spoon on the marinade. Cover and let marinate in a cool place for 4–6 hours.

4 Drain the fish when you are ready to cook it on the grill. Use the marinade to baste the fish occasionally during cooking.

COOK'S TIP

Keep the discarded herb stems to throw onto the coals when you cook, to add an extra dimension to the flavor.

Spicy Yogurt Marinade for Chicken

PLAN THIS DISH WELL in advance; the extra-long marinating time is necessary to develop a really mellow spicy flavor.

Serves 6

INGREDIENTS

6 chicken pieces
juice of 1 lemon
1 teaspoon salt
fresh mint, lemon and lime, to garnish

For the yogurt marinade

1 teaspoon coriander seeds
2 teaspoons cumin seeds
6 cloves
2 bay leaves
1 onion, quartered
2 garlic cloves
2-inch piece fresh ginger root, peeled and roughly chopped
½ teaspoon chili powder
1 teaspoon turmeric
⅔ cup plain yogurt

1 Skin the chicken joints and make deep slashes in the fleshiest parts with a sharp knife. Sprinkle on the lemon juice and salt, and rub in.

2 Make the marinade. Spread the coriander and cumin seeds, cloves and bay leaves in the bottom of a large frying pan and dry-fry over medium heat until the bay leaves are crispy.

3 Let the spice mixture cool, then grind it coarsely in a mortar and pestle.

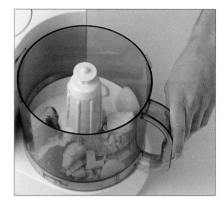

4 Finely mince the onion, garlic and ginger in a food processor or blender with the ground spices, chili powder, turmeric and yogurt. Strain in the lemon juice from the chicken.

5 Arrange the chicken in a single layer in a roasting pan. Pour on the marinade, then cover and chill for 24–36 hours, turning the chicken pieces occasionally.

6 Preheat the oven to 400°F. Cook the chicken for 45 minutes or until the juices run clear when the meat is pierced. Serve hot or cold, garnished with fresh mint and slices of lemon or lime.

VARIATION

This marinade will also work well brushed on skewers of lamb or pork fillet prior to grilling or broiling.

Lavender Balsamic Marinade for Lamb

LAVENDER IS AN UNUSUAL flavor to use with meat, but its heady, summery scent works well with lamb. Use the flower heads as garnish.

Serves 4

INGREDIENTS

4 racks of lamb, with 3–4 cutlets each

For the balsamic marinade
1 shallot, finely chopped
3 tablespoons chopped fresh lavender
1 tablespoon balsamic vinegar
2 tablespoons olive oil
1 tablespoon lemon juice
handful of lavender sprigs
salt and ground black pepper

1 Place the racks of lamb in a large mixing bowl or wide dish and sprinkle on the chopped shallot.

2 Sprinkle the chopped fresh lavender onto the lamb in the bowl.

3 Beat together the vinegar, olive oil and lemon juice and pour them onto the lamb. Season well with salt and ground black pepper and then turn the meat to coat evenly.

4 Sprinkle a few lavender sprigs on the broiler pan or on the coals of a medium-hot grill. Cook the lamb for 15–20 minutes, turning once and basting with any remaining marinade, until golden brown on the outside and still slightly pink in the center. Just before serving, garnish with lavender flower heads.

Red Wine and Juniper Marinade for Lamb

3 Preheat the oven to 325°F. Heat the oil in a pan and fry the meat and vegetables in batches until lightly browned. Transfer to a casserole and pour in the reserved marinade and stock. Cover and cook for 2 hours.

JUNIPER BERRIES HAVE A pungent flavor that is ideal to flavor lamb.

Serves 4–6

INGREDIENTS

1½-pound boned leg of lamb, trimmed and
  cut into 1-inch cubes
2 carrots, cut into batons
8 ounces baby onions or shallots
1½ cups button mushrooms
2 tablespoons vegetable oil
⅔ cup stock
2 tablespoons beurre manié
salt and ground black pepper

For the red wine and juniper marinade

4 rosemary sprigs
8 dried juniper berries, lightly crushed
8 black peppercorns, lightly crushed
1¼ cups red wine

1 Place the meat in a bowl, add the vegetables, rosemary, berries and peppercorns, then pour in the wine. Cover and set in a cool place for 4–5 hours, stirring once or twice during this time.

2 Remove the lamb and vegetables with a slotted spoon and set aside. Strain the marinade into a bowl.

4 Twenty minutes before the end of cooking, stir in the beurre manié, then cover and return to the oven. Season to taste before serving.

COOK'S TIP

Beurre manié is made of equal parts of butter and flour blended together. It is used as a thickening agent and should be added a small piece at a time.

Lemon and Rosemary Marinade for Lamb

MARINATE THE leg of lamb overnight in the refrigerator so that the flavors have plenty of time to penetrate the meat fully.

Serves 6

INGREDIENTS

3–3½-pound leg of lamb
2 garlic cloves, sliced
1 tablespoon cornstarch

For the lemon and rosemary marinade

1 lemon, sliced
6 rosemary sprigs
4 lemon thyme sprigs
1¼ cups dry white wine
4 tablespoons olive oil
salt and ground black pepper

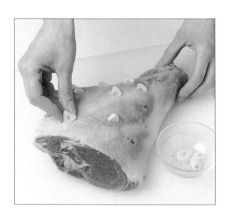

1 Make small cuts all over the surface of the lamb. Insert a garlic piece in each.

2 Place the lamb in a pan, with the lemon slices and herbs sprinkled on it.

3 Mix the wine, oil and seasoning and pour onto the lamb. Cover and set in a cool place for 4–6 hours, turning occasionally.

4 Preheat the oven to 350°F, then roast the lamb for 25 minutes per 1 pound plus another 25 minutes. Baste with the marinade.

VARIATION

You can also use lemon and rosemary marinade for chicken pieces, but you must roast the meat without the marinade, or it will become tough. Use the marinade for making into gravy when the chicken is cooked.

5 When the lamb is cooked, transfer to a warmed plate to rest. Drain the excess fat from the pan. Blend the cornstarch with a little cold water and stir into the juices. Stir over medium heat for 2–3 minutes, then adjust the seasoning.

Chinese Sesame Marinade for Beef Strips

TOASTED SESAME SEEDS BRING their distinctive smoky aroma to this Asian marinade.

Serves 4

INGREDIENTS

1 pound rump steak

2 tablespoons sesame seeds

1 tablespoon sesame oil

2 tablespoons vegetable oil

1½ cups small mushrooms, quartered

1 large bell green pepper, seeded and diced

4 scallions, chopped diagonally

For the Chinese sesame marinade

2 teaspoons cornstarch

2 tablespoons rice wine or sherry

1 tablespoon lemon juice

1 tablespoon soy sauce

few drops Tabasco sauce

1-inch piece fresh ginger root, peeled and grated

1 garlic clove, crushed

VARIATION

This marinade would also be good with lean pork fillet or chicken breast.

1 To make the marinade, blend the cornstarch with the rice wine or sherry. Add the other marinade ingredients. Trim the steak and cut into thin strips about ½ x 2 inches. Stir into the marinade, cover and set in a cool place for 3–4 hours.

2 Place the sesame seeds in a large frying pan or wok. Cook dry over medium heat, shaking the pan until the seeds are golden. Set aside.

3 Heat the oils in the frying pan. Drain the beef, reserving the marinade, and brown a few pieces at a time. Remove with a slotted spoon.

4 Add the mushrooms and pepper and fry for 2–3 minutes, stirring continuously. Add the scallions and cook for another minute.

5 Add the beef and reserved marinade, and stir over medium heat for 2 minutes or until evenly coated with the glaze. Sprinkle with the toasted sesame seeds, and serve.

Winter-spiced Ale Marinade for Beef

THIS MARINADE can also be used in a casserole of beef or lamb pieces. It will imbue the meat with a great flavor.

Serves 6

INGREDIENTS

3-pound top rump beef

For the winter-spiced ale marinade

1 onion, sliced

2 carrots, sliced

2 celery stalks, sliced

2–3 parsley stems, lightly crushed

large fresh thyme sprig

2 bay leaves

6 cloves, lightly crushed

1 cinnamon stick

8 black peppercorns

1¼ cups brown ale

3 tablespoons vegetable oil

2 tablespoons beurre manié

salt and ground black pepper

4 Preheat the oven to 325°F.

5 Return the vegetables to the casserole and pour the reserved marinade onto the beef.

6 Cover the casserole and bake for 2½ hours. Turn the beef two or three times in the marinade during cooking.

7 To serve, remove the beef and slice neatly. Arrange on a plate with the vegetables. Gradually stir the beurre manié into the marinade and cook until thickened. Adjust the seasoning.

COOK'S TIP

A rich, dark brown ale has the ideal flavor for this recipe, but the choice depends on your own taste.

1 Put the meat in a plastic bag placed inside a large, deep bowl. Add the vegetables, herbs and spices, then pour on the ale. Seal the bag and set in a cool place for 5–6 hours.

2 Remove the beef and set aside. Strain the marinade into a bowl, reserving the marinade.

3 Heat the oil in a flameproof casserole. Fry the vegetables until lightly browned, then remove with a slotted spoon and set aside. Brown the beef all over in the remaining oil.

Sauces for Sweet Dishes

Hot and cold sweet sauces can transform a simple scoop of ice cream or a piece of fruit into a complete dessert. A good range of sweet sauces can increase your repertoire of desserts three or four times over. Whether it's a tangy fruit coulis, a rich chocolate sauce, foaming sabayon or creamy custard, you can mix and match your favorite desserts with sauces to create a new dish every time.

Try a generous drizzle of Chocolate Sauce on profiteroles for a perfectly indulgent treat, then next time spoon it on your favorite vanilla ice cream. Or, for a lighter, less calorie-laden treat, how about Maple Yogurt Sauce with Poached Pears?

It's worth making the most of fruit in season to make deliciously fresh fruit coulis to use in creative combinations at any time of year. Broiled pineapple is irresistible with a luscious spoonful of Papaya Sauce, or try Passion Fruit Coulis spooned on scoops of frozen yogurt.

For a more traditional partnership, try Toffee Sauce poured on Hot Date Puddings or old-fashioned British Castle Puddings with Custard.

Papaya Dip with Fresh Fruit

SWEET AND SMOOTH PAPAYA teams up well with crème fraîche to make a luscious, tropical sweet dip which is very good with cookies or fresh fruit for dipping. If fresh coconut is not available, buy dry, shredded coconut and lightly toast until golden.

Serves 6

INGREDIENTS

2 ripe papayas
scant 1 cup crème fraîche
1 piece stem ginger
fresh coconut, to decorate
papaya or other fresh fruit, to serve

1 Halve the papayas lengthwise, then scoop out and discard the seeds.

2 Scoop out the flesh and process it until smooth in a food processor or blender.

3 Stir in the crème fraîche and process until well blended. Finely chop the stem ginger and stir it in, then chill until ready to serve.

4 Pierce a hole in the "eye" of the coconut and drain the liquid. Put the coconut in a plastic bag. Hold it securely in one hand and hit it sharply with a hammer.

5 Remove the shell from a piece of coconut, then snap the nut into pieces no wider than 1 inch.

6 Use a swivel-bladed vegetable peeler to shave off ¾-inch lengths of coconut. Sprinkle these on the dip. Serve with pieces of extra papaya or other fresh fruit.

Malted Chocolate and Banana Dip with Fresh Fruit

CHOCOLATE AND BANANA combine irresistibly in this rich dip, served with fresh fruit in season. For a creamier dip, stir in some lightly whipped cream just before serving.

Serves 4

INGREDIENTS

2 ounces semi-sweet chocolate
2 large ripe bananas
1 tablespoon malt extract
mixed fresh fruit, such as strawberries, peaches and kiwi fruit, halved or sliced, to serve

1 Break the chocolate into pieces and place in a small, heatproof bowl. Stand the bowl over a pan of gently simmering water and stir the chocolate occasionally until it melts. Let cool slightly.

2 Break the bananas into pieces and process in a food processor or blender until finely chopped.

3 With the motor running, pour in the malt extract, and continue processing the mixture until it is thick and frothy.

4 Drizzle in the chocolate in a steady stream and process until well blended. Serve immediately, with the prepared fruit alongside.

COOK'S TIP

This smooth dip can be prepared in advance and chilled.

Passion Fruit Coulis with Yogurt Sundaes

FROZEN YOGURT makes a refreshing change from ice cream. Here, it is partnered with a delicious fresh fruit coulis that is simple to make. Fresh summer strawberries are unlikely to need sweetening, but some varieties may need a little sugar.

Serves 4

INGREDIENTS

1 1/2 cups strawberries, hulled
   and halved
2 ripe peaches, pitted and chopped
8 scoops (about 12 ounces) vanilla or strawberry frozen yogurt

For the passion fruit coulis

1 1/2 cups strawberries, hulled
   and halved
1 passion fruit
2 teaspoons confectioners' sugar (optional)

1 To make the coulis, purée the strawberries. Scoop out the passion fruit pulp and add it to the coulis. Sweeten with confectioners' sugar if necessary.

2 Spoon half the remaining strawberries and half the chopped peaches into four tall sundae glasses.

3 Add a scoop of frozen yogurt. Set aside a few choice pieces of fruit for decoration, and use the rest to make another layer on top of each sundae. Top each with a final scoop of frozen yogurt.

4 Pour on the passion fruit coulis, and decorate the sundaes with the reserved strawberries and pieces of peach. Serve immediately.

Hazelnut Dip with Fruit Fondue

FRESH FRUIT IS ALWAYS a good choice for a colorful, simple dessert, and this recipe makes it complete, with a delicious sauce for dipping. Any fruit that can be served raw can be used for this dish. Try to use fruits in a range of different colors for an attractive presentation.

Serves 2

INGREDIENTS

selection of fresh fruits, such as satsumas,
   kiwi fruit, grapes, cape gooseberries and
   whole strawberries

For the hazelnut dip

1/4 cup cream cheese
2/3 cup hazelnut or plain yogurt
1 teaspoon vanilla extract
1 teaspoon sugar
1/3 cup shelled hazelnuts, chopped

1 First prepare the fruits. Peel and segment the satsumas. Then peel the kiwi fruit and cut into wedges. Wash the grapes and peel back the papery casing on the cape gooseberries.

2 To make the dip, beat the cream cheese with the yogurt, vanilla and sugar in a bowl. Stir in three-quarters of the hazelnuts.

3 Spoon into a glass serving dish set on a platter or into small pots on individual plates and sprinkle the remaining hazelnuts on top. Arrange the prepared fruits around the dip and serve immediately.

Lemon and Lime Sauce with Crépes

THIS IS A TANGY, refreshing sauce and is a perfect foil for the pancakes.

Serves 4

INGREDIENTS

scant 1 cup all-purpose flour
pinch of salt
1 egg
1¼ cups milk
vegetable oil, for frying
lemon balm or mint, to decorate

For the lemon and lime sauce

1 lemon
2 limes
¼ cup sugar
1½ tablespoons arrowroot
1¼ cups water

1 First, make the sauce. Using a citrus zester, peel the zests thinly from the lemon and limes taking care not to cut into the pith. Squeeze the juice from the fruit. Place the zest in a pan, cover with water and bring to a boil.

2 Drain through a sieve and reserve the zest.

3 In a small bowl, mix a little sugar with the arrowroot. Blend in enough water to make a smooth paste. Heat the remaining water, pour in the arrowroot mixture, and stir continuously until the sauce boils and thickens. Stir in the remaining sugar, citrus juice and reserved zest. Keep the sauce hot while you make the crépes.

4 Sift the dry ingredients into a bowl and make a well in the center. Add the egg and beat in with a wooden spoon. Beat in the milk, drawing in the flour to make a smooth batter.

5 Heat a little oil in a large, heavy frying pan. When hot, pour in a thin layer of batter and cook for 1–2 minutes or until set. Toss the crépe and cook the other side until golden brown. Transfer the crépe to a plate and keep it warm while you make the rest of the crépes.

6 Serve with the hot sauce and decorate with lemon balm or mint.

Butterscotch Sauce with Waffles

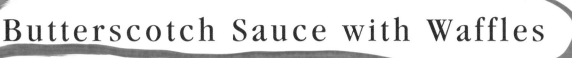

THIS IS A DELICIOUSLY sweet sauce that will be loved by everyone.

Serves 4–6

INGREDIENTS

1 package ready-made waffles
vanilla ice cream, to serve

For the butterscotch sauce
6 tablespoons butter
³/₄ cup dark brown sugar
³/₄ cup evaporated milk
¹/₃ cup hazelnuts

1 Warm the waffles in a preheated oven, according to the package instructions, while you make the butterscotch sauce.

2 Melt the butter and sugar in a heavy pan, bring to a boil and boil for 2 minutes. Cool for 5 minutes.

3 Heat the evaporated milk to just below the boiling point, then gradually stir into the sugar mixture. Cook over low heat for 2 minutes, stirring the sauce frequently.

4 Spread the hazelnuts on a baking sheet and toast under a hot broiler until golden brown. Put on a clean dish towel and rub briskly to remove the skins.

5 Chop the nuts roughly and stir into the sauce. Serve the sauce hot, poured over scoops of vanilla ice cream and the warm waffles.

VARIATION

Substitute any nut for the hazelnuts. Pecans, for example, add a luxurious flavor. You could also add plump, juicy raisins and a dash of rum instead of the nuts.

Maple and Cointreau Syrup with Oranges

THE MAPLE SYRUP MAKES this one of the most delicious ways to eat an orange. For an alcohol-free version, simply omit the Cointreau or Grand Marnier.

Serves 4

INGREDIENTS

melted butter, for brushing
4 medium oranges
crème fraîche or fromage frais, to serve

For the maple and Cointreau syrup
2 tablespoons maple syrup
2 tablespoons Cointreau or Grand
  Marnier liqueur
4 teaspoons butter

1 Preheat the oven to 400°F. Cut four double-thick squares of aluminum foil, large enough to wrap each of the oranges. Brush the center of each square of foil with plenty of melted butter.

2 Remove some shreds of orange zest, to decorate. Blanch these, dry them and set them aside.

3 Peel all of the oranges, removing all the white pith and catching the juice in a bowl.

4 Slice each of the oranges crosswise into thick slices. Reassemble the slices and place each stack on a square of double thick aluminum foil.

5 Tuck the foil up securely around the reassembled oranges to keep them in shape, leaving the foil parcels open at the top.

6 To make the syrup, mix the reserved orange juice, maple syrup and liqueur and spoon the mixture onto the oranges.

7 Add a pat of butter to each parcel and close the foil at the top to seal in the juices. Place the parcels in the oven for 10–12 minutes or until hot. (The parcels can also be cooked on a hot grill, if desired.) Serve with crème fraîche or fromage frais, topped with the reserved shreds of orange zest.

Hot Plum Sauce with Floating Islands

THE PLUM SAUCE CAN be made in advance, then reheated just before you cook the meringues. This is a delicious dish that is simpler to make than it looks.

Serves 4

INGREDIENTS

2 egg whites
2 tablespoons concentrated apple juice syrup
freshly grated nutmeg

For the hot plum sauce
1 pound red plums
1¼ cups apple juice

1 To make the plum sauce, halve the plums and remove the pits. Place them in a wide saucepan, with the apple juice.

2 Bring to a boil and then cover with a lid and let simmer gently for 15–20 minutes or until the plums are tender.

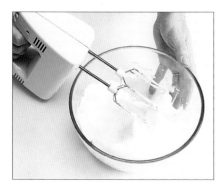

3 Meanwhile, place the egg whites in a clean, dry bowl and whisk them until they hold soft peaks.

4 Gradually whisk in the apple juice syrup, whisking until the meringue holds fairly firm peaks.

5 Using a tablespoon, scoop the meringue mixture into the gently simmering plum sauce. You may need to cook the "islands" in two batches.

6 Cover and let simmer gently for 2–3 minutes or until the meringues are just set.

7 Serve immediately, sprinkled with a little freshly grated nutmeg.

Custard with Castle Puddings

THIS TRADITIONAL British dessert is served with one of the most traditional sweet sauces—a really creamy vanilla custard.

Serves 4

INGREDIENTS

about 3 tablespoons berry jam
½ cup butter
generous ½ cup sugar
2 eggs, beaten
few drops of vanilla extract
generous 1 cup self-rising flour

For the custard

4 eggs
1½–2 tablespoons sugar
scant 2 cups milk
few drops of vanilla extract

1 Preheat the oven to 350°F. Butter four dariole molds. Put about 2 teaspoons jam in the bottom of each mold.

2 Beat the butter and sugar together until light and fluffy, then gradually beat in the eggs, beating well after each addition and adding the vanilla toward the end.

3 Lightly fold in the flour, then divide the mixture among the molds.

4 Bake the puddings for about 20 minutes, until well risen and a light golden color.

5 Meanwhile, make the custard. Whisk the eggs and sugar together. Bring the milk to a boil in a heavy saucepan, preferably nonstick, then slowly pour onto the sweetened egg mixture, stirring constantly.

6 Return the milk and egg mixture to the pan and heat very gently, stirring, until the mixture thickens enough to coat the back of a spoon; do not let boil. Stir in the vanilla. Cover the pan and remove from heat.

7 Remove the molds from the oven, let stand for a few minutes, then turn the puddings onto warmed plates and serve with the hot custard.

COOK'S TIPS

• If you prefer, instead of baking the puddings, you can cover and steam them for 30–40 minutes.
• If you do not have dariole molds, use ramekins.
• Make sure you buy real vanilla and not the artificial flavoring. You will only need a drop or two.

Toffee Sauce with Hot Date Puddings

THIS TOFFEE SAUCE IS A great standby for hot or cold desserts. It is equally delicious served with poached apple or pear slices, spooned onto ice cream or drizzled on a hot steamed pudding.

Serves 6

INGREDIENTS

¼ cup butter, softened

6 tablespoons light brown sugar

2 eggs, beaten

1 cup self-rising flour

½ teaspoon baking soda

generous 1 cup fresh dates, peeled, pitted and chopped

5 tablespoons boiling water

2 teaspoons coffee extract

For the toffee sauce

6 tablespoons light brown sugar

¼ cup butter

4 tablespoons heavy cream

2 tablespoons brandy

1 Preheat the oven to 350°F. Place a baking sheet in the oven to heat up. Grease six individual pudding molds.

2 Cream the butter and sugar in a large mixing bowl until pale and fluffy. Gradually add the beaten eggs a little at a time, beating well after each addition.

3 Sift the flour and baking soda together and fold into the creamed mixture.

4 Put the dates in a heatproof bowl, pour on the boiling water and mash with a potato masher. Add the coffee extract, then stir the paste into the creamed mixture.

COOK'S TIP

It is preferable to peel the dates, as the skins can be rather tough: simply squeeze them between your thumb and forefinger and the skins will pop off.

5 Spoon the mixture into the prepared molds. Place on the hot baking sheet and bake for 20 minutes.

6 To make the toffee sauce, put all the ingredients in a pan and heat gently, stirring until smooth.

7 Increase the heat and boil for 1 minute. Turn the warm puddings out onto individual dessert plates. Spoon a generous amount of sauce on each and serve immediately.

Banana Sauce with Chocolate Cinnamon Cake

THIS CREAMY BANANA SAUCE makes a simple chocolate cake into a really luxurious dessert that is suitable for any special occasion.

Serves 6

INGREDIENTS

7 tablespoons unsalted butter, at room temperature, plus extra for greasing

4 ounces semi-sweet chocolate, finely chopped

1 tablespoon instant coffee powder

5 eggs, separated

1 cup sugar

1 cup all-purpose flour

2 teaspoons ground cinnamon

For the banana sauce

4 ripe bananas

¼ cup light brown sugar

1 tablespoon fresh lemon juice

¾ cup whipping cream

1 tablespoon rum (optional)

1 Preheat the oven to 350°F. Grease an 8-inch round cake pan.

2 Combine the chocolate and butter in a heatproof bowl set over hot water or in the top of a double boiler. Stir until melted. Remove from heat and stir in the coffee. Set aside.

3 Beat the egg yolks together with the sugar until thick and lemon-colored. Add the chocolate mixture and beat on low speed just to blend evenly.

4 Sift together the flour and ground cinnamon into a bowl. In another bowl, beat the egg whites until they hold stiff peaks.

5 Fold a dollop of whites into the chocolate mixture to lighten it. Fold in the remaining whites in three batches, alternating with the sifted flour.

6 Pour the cake mixture into the prepared pan.

7 Bake the cake for 40–50 minutes or until a skewer inserted in the center comes out clean. Turn out the cake onto a wire rack.

8 Meanwhile, make the sauce. Preheat the broiler. Slice the bananas into a shallow, heatproof dish. Add the brown sugar and lemon juice and stir to blend. Place under the broiler and cook, stirring occasionally, for about 8 minutes or until the sugar is caramelized and bubbling.

9 Transfer the bananas to a bowl and mash with a fork until almost smooth. Stir in the cream and rum, if using. Cut the chocolate cake into slices and serve it warm, with the banana sauce.

VARIATION

For a special occasion, top the cake slices with a scoop of ice cream (rum and raisin, chocolate or vanilla) before adding the sauce. With this addition, the dessert will serve at least 8.

Berry Sauce with Baked Ricotta Cakes

THE FLAVOR OF THIS fragrant fruity sauce contrasts well with these honey and vanilla-flavored desserts.

Serves 4

INGREDIENTS

generous 1 cup ricotta cheese

2 egg whites, beaten

about 4 tablespoons honey

few drops of vanilla extract

fresh mint leaves, to decorate (optional)

For the red berry sauce

4 cups mixed fresh or frozen
    fruit, such as strawberries, raspberries,
    blackberries and cherries

COOK'S TIPS

• The sauce can be made a day ahead. Chill until ready to use.

• Frozen fruit doesn't need extra water, as there will be ice crystals clinging to the berries.

Preheat the oven to 350°F.

2 Place the ricotta cheese in a bowl and break it up with a wooden spoon. Add the beaten egg whites, honey and vanilla and mix thoroughly until the mixture is smooth and well combined.

3 Lightly grease four ramekins. Spoon the ricotta mixture into the prepared ramekins and level the tops. Bake for 20 minutes or until the ricotta cakes are risen and golden.

4 Meanwhile, make the berry sauce. Reserve about a quarter of the fruit for decoration. Place the rest of the fruit in a saucepan, with a little water if the fruit is fresh, and heat gently until softened. Let cool slightly, remove any cherry pits, if using cherries.

5 Press the fruit through a sieve, then taste and sweeten with honey if it is too tart. Serve the sauce, warm or cold, with the ricotta cakes. Decorate with the reserved berries and mint leaves, if using.

Calvados and Chocolate Sauce with Frozen Pear Terrine

THIS RICH CHOCOLATE SAUCE would complement vanilla ice cream for a simpler dessert.

Serves 8

INGREDIENTS

3–3½ pounds ripe William's pears
juice of 1 lemon
generous ½ cup sugar
10 whole cloves
julienne strips of orange zest, to decorate

For the Calvados and chocolate sauce

7 ounces semi-sweet chocolate
4 tablespoons hot strong black coffee
scant 1 cup heavy cream
2 tablespoons Calvados or brandy

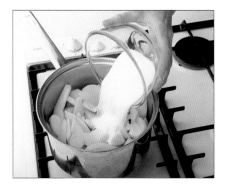

1 Peel, core and slice the pears. Place in a pan with the lemon juice, sugar, cloves and 6 tablespoons water. Cover and simmer for 10 minutes. Remove the cloves. Let cool.

2 Process the pears with their juice and pour the purée into a freezer-proof bowl. Cover and freeze until firm.

3 Line a 2-pound loaf pan with plastic wrap. Let the plastic wrap overhang the sides of the pan. Remove the frozen pear purée from the freezer and spoon it into a food processor. Process until smooth. Pour into the prepared pan, cover and freeze until firm.

4 To make the sauce, break the chocolate into a large, heatproof bowl. Place the bowl over a saucepan of hot water and let melt.

5 Stir the coffee into the melted chocolate until smooth. Gradually stir in the cream and then the Calvados or brandy. Set aside.

6 About 20 minutes before serving, remove the pan from the freezer. Invert the terrine onto a plate, lift off the plastic wrap and place the terrine in the refrigerator to soften slightly. Warm the sauce over hot water.

7 Place a slice of terrine onto each dessert plate and spoon on some of the sauce. Decorate with julienne strips of orange zest and serve immediately.

COOK'S TIP

This is a good dish to prepare in advance for a dinner party, as the terrine will store successfully for a month in the freezer, but remember to remove it in time to soften slightly before serving.

Mexican Hot Fudge Sauce with Sundaes

DEFINITELY NOT ONE FOR dieters but best kept for those special, indulgent days!

Serves 4

INGREDIENTS

2½ cups vanilla ice cream
2½ cups coffee ice cream
2 large ripe bananas, sliced
whipped cream
toasted sliced almonds

For the hot fudge sauce

4 tablespoons light brown sugar
⅓ cup golden or corn syrup
3 tablespoons strong black coffee
1 teaspoon ground cinnamon
5 ounces dark chocolate, broken up
5 tablespoons whipping cream
3 tablespoons coffee liqueur (optional)

1 For the sauce, combine the sugar, golden syrup, coffee and cinnamon in a heavy saucepan. Bring to a boil. Boil the mixture, stirring constantly, for about 5 minutes.

COOK'S TIP

Use good quality, dark chocolate with at least 70% cocoa solids.

2 Remove from heat and stir in the chocolate. When melted and smooth, stir in the cream and liqueur, if using. Let the sauce cool just to lukewarm or, if made ahead, reheat gently while assembling the sundaes.

3 Using an ice cream scoop, fill the sundae dishes with 1 scoop each of vanilla and coffee ice cream.

4 Arrange the bananas on top of each dish. Pour the warm sauce onto the bananas.

5 Top each sundae with a generous rosette of whipped cream. Top with the toasted almonds and serve immediately.

Sabayon Sauce

THIS FROTHY SAUCE is very versatile and can be served alone with cookies or hot over cake, fruit or even ice cream. Never let the sauce stand before serving, as it will collapse.

Serves 4–6

INGREDIENTS

1 egg
2 egg yolks
scant ½ cup sugar
⅔ cup Marsala or other sweet white wine
finely grated zest and juice of 1 lemon
cookies, to serve

1 Put the egg, yolks and sugar into a medium bowl and whisk until they are pale and thick.

2 Stand the bowl over a saucepan of hot, but not boiling, water. Gradually add the Marsala or white wine and lemon juice, a little at a time, whisking vigorously.

3 Continue whisking until it is thick enough to leave a trail.

COOK'S TIP

A generous pinch of arrowroot whisked together with the egg yolks and sugar will prevent the sauce from collapsing too quickly.

4 To serve the sabayon cold, place it over a bowl of ice water and continue whisking until chilled. Add the finely grated lemon zest and stir in. Pour into small glasses and serve immediately, with the cookies.

Chocolate Sauce with Profiteroles

A REAL TREAT IF you're not counting calories, this sauce is also good with scoops of vanilla ice cream.

Serves 6

INGREDIENTS
9 tablespoons all-purpose flour

¼ cup butter

⅔ cup water

2 eggs, lightly beaten

⅔ cup whipping cream, whipped

For the chocolate sauce

⅔ cup heavy cream

¼ cup butter

¼ cup vanilla sugar

6 ounces semi-sweet chocolate

2 tablespoons brandy

VARIATION

White chocolate and orange sauce

3 tablespoons sugar, to replace vanilla sugar

finely grated zest of 1 orange

6 ounces white chocolate, to replace semi-sweet chocolate

2 tablespoons orange liqueur, to replace brandy

1 Make the chocolate sauce. Heat the cream with the butter and vanilla sugar in a bowl over a saucepan of hot water. Stir until smooth, then cool.

2 Break the chocolate into the cream. Stir until it is melted and thoroughly combined.

3 Stir in the brandy a little at a time, then let the sauce cool to room temperature.

4 For the white chocolate and orange sauce, heat the cream and butter with the sugar and orange zest in the top of a double boiler, until dissolved. Use the white chocolate instead of semi-sweet chocolate in step 2, and orange liqueur instead of the brandy in step 3.

5 To make the profiteroles, preheat the oven to 400°F. Sift the flour onto a plate. Melt the butter and water in a saucepan and bring to a boil.

6 Remove the saucepan from heat and add the flour all at once. Beat with a wooden spoon until smooth. Cool for 1–2 minutes, then gradually beat in enough egg to give a piping consistency. Beat well until glossy. Pipe small balls of the mixture onto dampened baking sheets.

7 Bake 15–20 minutes or until crisp. Make a slit in the sides and cool on a wire rack.

8 Fill a piping bag with cream and pipe some into each profiterole. Pile onto a plate, topped with a little sauce. Serve the remaining chocolate sauce separately.

Papaya Sauce with Broiled Pineapple

TRY THE PAPAYA SAUCE with savory dishes, too. It tastes great with grilled chicken and game birds as well as pork and lamb.

Serves 6

INGREDIENTS

I sweet pineapple
melted butter, for greasing and brushing
2 pieces drained stem ginger in syrup, cut into fine matchsticks
2 tablespoons sugar
pinch of ground cinnamon
2 tablespoons stem ginger syrup
fresh mint sprigs, to decorate

For the papaya sauce
I ripe papaya, peeled and seeded
¾ cup apple juice

I Peel the pineapple and take spiral slices off the outside to remove the eyes. Cut it crosswise into six slices, each I inch thick.

2 Line a baking sheet with a sheet of aluminum foil, rolling up the sides to make a rim. Grease the foil with melted butter. Preheat the broiler.

VARIATION

If desired, substitute half apple juice and half papaya nectar for the apple juice in the sauce.

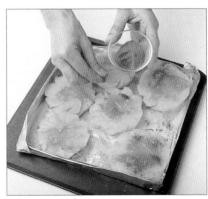

3 Arrange the pineapple slices on the baking sheet. Brush with butter, then top with the ginger matchsticks, sugar and cinnamon. Drizzle on the stem ginger syrup. Broil for 5–7 minutes or until the slices are lightly charred.

4 Cut a few slices from the papaya and set aside, then purée the rest together with the apple juice in a food processor or blender.

5 Press the purée through a sieve placed over a bowl, then stir in any juices from cooking the pineapple.

6 Serve the pineapple slices with a little sauce drizzled around each plate. Decorate with the reserved papaya slices and the mint sprigs.

quelconque

Nectarine Sauce with Latticed Peaches

MAKE THIS IN SUMMER **when the fruits are in season and enjoy the fresh flavor.**

Serves 6

INGREDIENTS

For the pastry

1 cup all-purpose flour

3 tablespoons butter or sunflower margarine

3 tablespoons plain yogurt

2 tablespoons orange juice

milk, for brushing

For the filling

3 ripe peaches or nectarines

3 tablespoons ground almonds

2 tablespoons low-fat plain yogurt

finely grated zest of 1 small orange

¼ teaspoon natural almond extract

For the nectarine sauce

1 ripe nectarine or peach

3 tablespoons orange juice

1 For the pastry, sift the flour into a bowl and, using your fingertips, rub in the butter or margarine. Stir in the yogurt and orange juice to bind the mixture into a firm dough.

2 Roll out about half the pastry thinly, and use a cookie cutter to stamp out rounds of about 3 inches in diameter, or slightly larger than the circumference of the peaches. Place on a lightly greased baking sheet.

3 Skin the peaches or nectarines, halve them and remove the pits.

4 Mix the almonds, yogurt, orange zest and almond extract. Spoon into each peach half and place, cut side down, onto the pastry rounds.

5 Roll out the remaining pastry thinly and cut into thin strips. Arrange the strips onto the peaches to form a lattice, brushing with milk to secure firmly. Trim off the ends neatly.

6 Chill in the refrigerator for 30 minutes. Preheat the oven to 400°F. Brush the tarts with milk, and bake for 15–18 minutes.

7 For the sauce, skin the nectarine or peach and remove the pit. Purée it in a food processor, with the orange juice. Serve the peaches hot, with the sauce spooned around.

COOK'S TIP

To peel peaches, blanch them in boiling water for about 30 seconds then place in ice water. The skins will slip off.

Lime and Cardamom Sauce with Bananas

THE WARM SPICY-SWEET FLAVOR of cardamom is offset by the tang of lime in this unusual sauce.

Serves 4

INGREDIENTS

6 small bananas
2 tablespoons butter
vanilla ice cream, to serve

For the lime and cardamom sauce
2 tablespoons butter
seeds from 4 cardamom pods, crushed
½ cup sliced almonds
thinly pared zest and juice of 2 limes
¼ cup light brown sugar
2 tablespoons dark rum

1 Peel the bananas and cut them in half lengthwise. Heat the butter in a large frying pan. Add half the bananas, and cook until the undersides are golden. Turn carefully, using a spatula.

2 As they cook, transfer the bananas to a heatproof serving dish. Cook the remaining bananas in the same way.

VARIATION

If you prefer not to use alcohol in your cooking, replace the rum with orange juice or even pineapple juice.

3 To make the lime and cardamom sauce melt the butter, then add the cardamom seeds and almonds. Cook, stirring, until golden.

4 Stir in the lime zest and juice, then the sugar. Cook, stirring, until the mixture is smooth, bubbling and slightly reduced. Stir in the rum.

5 Pour the sauce onto the bananas and serve immediately, with vanilla ice cream.

COOK'S TIP

Crush the cardamom seeds in a mortar and pestle just before using, to retain their essential flavor.

Maple Yogurt Sauce with Poached Pears

THE SWEET-SOUR TASTE OF the maple syrup and yogurt will partner most poached fruit but is especially good with pears. Choose a firm but ripe pear such as Conference.

Serves 4

INGREDIENTS

4 firm pears
1 tablespoon lemon juice
1 cup sweet white wine
  or cider
thinly pared zest of 1 lemon
1 cinnamon stick

For the maple yogurt sauce
pear cooking liquid
2 tablespoons maple syrup
½ teaspoon arrowroot
⅔ cup plain yogurt

3 Add the lemon zest and cinnamon stick and bring to a boil. Reduce the heat, cover the pan and simmer gently for 30–40 minutes or until the pears are tender. Turn the pears occasionally so that they cook evenly. Lift out the pears carefully, draining them.

4 To make the sauce, bring the liquid to a boil and boil uncovered to reduce it to about 7 tablespoons. Strain and add the maple syrup. Blend a little with the arrowroot. Return to the pan and cook, stirring, until thick. Cool.

5 Slice each cored pear about three-quarters of the way through, leaving the slices attached at the stem end. Fan out on a serving plate.

6 Stir 2 tablespoons of the cooled syrup into the yogurt and spoon it around the pears. Drizzle with the remaining syrup and serve immediately.

1 Thinly peel the pears, leaving them whole and with stems. Brush them with lemon juice, to prevent them from browning. Use a potato peeler or small knife to scoop out the core from the base of each pear.

2 Place the pears in a wide, heavy saucepan and pour on the wine or cider, with enough cold water almost to cover the pears.

VARIATION

If you want to make this sauce for another dessert, substitute fruit juice for the pear cooking liquid in step 4.

Strawberry Sauce with Lemon Hearts

THIS SPEEDY SWEET SAUCE makes a delicious accompaniment for these delicate lemon and cheese hearts.

Serves 4

INGREDIENTS

¾ cup ricotta cheese
⅔ cup plain yogurt
1 tablespoon sugar
finely grated zest of ½ lemon
2 tablespoons lemon juice
2 teaspoons powdered gelatin
2 egg whites
oil, for greasing

For the strawberry sauce

2 cups fresh or frozen and thawed
    strawberries, plus extra
    to decorate
1 tablespoon lemon juice

1 Beat the ricotta until smooth. Stir in the yogurt, sugar and lemon zest.

2 Place the lemon juice in a small bowl and sprinkle on the gelatin. Place the bowl over a pan of hot water and stir the mixture to dissolve the gelatin completely.

3 Beat the egg whites until they form soft peaks. Quickly stir the gelatin into the ricotta cheese mixture, mixing it in evenly, then immediately fold in the beaten egg whites.

4 Spoon the mixture into four lightly oiled, individual heart-shaped molds and chill the molds until set.

5 To make the sauce, place the strawberries and lemon juice in a food processor and process until smooth. Pour onto plates and top with turned-out hearts. Decorate with the extra strawberries.

VARIATION

Add a dash of Cointreau or Grand Marnier liqueur to the strawberry sauce.

Raspberry Sauce with Baked Peaches

PEACHES AND RASPBERRIES are classic partners—a combination that's hard to beat for a sophisticated summer dessert. Fresh nectarines can also be used instead of peaches. Try this sauce with a cool slice of melon for a summer appetizer.

Serves 6

INGREDIENTS

3 tablespoons unsalted butter, at
   room temperature

¼ cup sugar

1 egg, beaten

½ cup ground almonds

6 ripe peaches

For the raspberry sauce

1 cup raspberries

1 tablespoon confectioners' sugar

1 tablespoon fruit-flavored brandy
   (optional)

3 Place the peach halves on a baking sheet (secure with crumpled aluminum foil to keep them steady). Fill the hollow in each peach half with the butter and almond mixture.

4 Bake for about 30 minutes or until the almond filling is puffed and golden and the peaches are very tender.

5 For the sauce, combine all the ingredients in a food processor or blender. Add the reserved peach flesh. Process until smooth. Press through a strainer set over a bowl to remove fibers and seeds.

6 Let the peaches cool. Place two halves on each plate and spoon on the sauce. Serve immediately.

1 Preheat the oven to 350°F. Beat the butter with the sugar until soft and fluffy. Beat in the egg. Add the ground almonds and beat just to blend well together.

2 Halve the peaches and remove the pits. With a spoon, scrape out some of the flesh from each peach half, slightly enlarging the hollow left by the pit. Reserve the excess peach flesh to use in the sauce.

Index